From The Stick to The Cove

To Mark

Thanks

From The Stick to The Cove

My Six Decades with the San Francisco Giants

Mike Murphy with Chris Haft

Enjoy The Book
Mike Murphy
Go Giants
2021

TRIUMPH
BOOKS

Copyright © 2020 by Mike Murphy and Chris Haft

No part of this publication may be reproduced, stored in a retrieval system, or transmitted in any form by any means, electronic, mechanical, photocopying, or otherwise, without the prior written permission of the publisher, Triumph Books LLC, 814 North Franklin Street, Chicago, Illinois 60610.

Library of Congress Cataloging-in-Publication Data

Names: Murphy, Mike (Clubhouse manager), author. | Haft, Chris, author.
Title: From the stick to the cove : my six decades with the San Francisco Giants / By Mike Murphy with Chris Haft.
Description: Chicago, Illinois: Triumph Books, [2020] | Contents: Ring Ceremony—Willie Mays—2010—2012—2014—The Dynasty's top players, games and homers—Bruce Bochy—Nicknames and numbers—Joining the club—Celebrity encounters—Tributes to Murph. |
Summary: "This book chronicles Mike Murphy's long tenure with the San Francisco Giants"—Provided by publisher.
Identifiers: LCCN 2019058776 | ISBN 9781629377681 (paperback) | ISBN 9781641254069 (epub)
Subjects: LCSH: Murphy, Mike (Clubhouse manager) | San Francisco Giants (Baseball team)—History.
Classification: LCC GV865.M797 A3 2020 | DDC 796.357092 [B]—dc23
LC record available at https://lccn.loc.gov/2019058776

This book is available in quantity at special discounts for your group or organization. For further information, contact:

Triumph Books LLC
814 North Franklin Street
Chicago, Illinois 60610
(312) 337-0747
www.triumphbooks.com

Printed in U.S.A.
ISBN: 978-1-62937-768-1
Design by Nord Compo
Photos courtesy of AP Images unless otherwise indicated

*To my wonderful family,
who has put up with me through all these years.*
—MM

*This is for Samantha; Stephanie;
Mom; Auntie Annabella; Aunt Helene;
and perennial MVP, Uncle Larry.*
—CH

Contents

	Foreword *by Willie Mays* ix
1	Ring Ceremony. 1
2	Willie Mays 20
3	Joining the Club 47
4	Celebrity Encounters. 66
5	2010 85
6	Bruce Bochy 107
7	2012 126
8	Nicknames and Numbers 149
9	2014 171
10	The Dynasty's Top Players, Games, and Homers. 190
11	Tributes to Murph 206
	Acknowledgments 225

Foreword

IT WAS A TREAT FOR ME TO PLAY in the major leagues. There are 30 major league clubhouses, but only one has Mike Murphy in it. That's a big reason why the San Francisco Giants remain a special franchise. Since the Giants moved from New York to San Francisco—and I'm one of the handful of people still around who actually experienced that move—Mike Murphy is the only individual who has been continuously employed by the team.

First, he was a batboy at Seals Stadium, the Giants' first home in San Francisco. Then he became the visiting team's assistant clubhouse manager before he reached the age of 20. Shortly after that, we started playing home games at Candlestick Park. In 1980, some 20 years later, the guy we all call "Murph" rose to the position of Giants clubhouse manager, which is how most people will remember him. The Giants clubhouse was named the Mike Murphy Clubhouse in honor of his loyal and tireless service when the team moved into Pacific Bell Park, now known as Oracle Park, in 2000.

I don't worry too much about Murph. He's been able to take care of himself around ballplayers, it seems, from Day One—as well as taking care of them. Through the years I've taken increasing pride in Murph's reputation for reliability.

Most importantly, Murph's my friend. He's a good man. If you come to the Giants clubhouse for the first time, Murph will be the guy you look for. Murph, who's 77, stopped being a starry-eyed fan a long time ago. But I still laugh when I think about taking him to Frank Sinatra's house in Palm Springs, California, for dinner in the mid-1960s. It was a surprise visit for Murph, who loves Sinatra and his music more than anyone I know. Knowing what was in store for him, I kind of dropped little teasing hints as we drove to Frank's place. Referring to our host, who had more gold records than I've got awards, I told Murph shortly before we arrived, "I think you'll like him."

And everyone likes Murph, too. Before our home games at Seals Stadium, Murph did both clubhouses, and all the guys loved him. The clubbies and other staff people don't get as much money as they should, especially back in the day. That's why I told him, "If you don't have enough money to buy a suit or pants or something, you come to me." Believe me: he's paid me back tenfold.

Sometimes we would sit on the bench—just him and I—and talk. It was nothing special, just real talk that went beyond baseball. But baseball is his love, and he's also a good ambassador for the sport. He even represented the Giants one year at the amateur draft. He's been everywhere and done everything. Stick around to read about Murph and his fascinating career. I think you'll like him, too.

—*Willie Mays*

1

Ring Ceremony

FOR THE SAN FRANCISCO GIANTS, the 2010 World Series ring ceremony was a big, big, *big* deal. We had never won it all since the franchise moved West from New York, following the 1957 season—just three years after the Giants recorded a four-game World Series sweep of the Cleveland Indians. Historically, the Giants had many reasons to be proud of themselves. Our greatness was embodied in our six living Hall of Famers—Willie Mays, Willie McCovey, Juan Marichal, Gaylord Perry, Orlando Cepeda, and Monte Irvin. We represented class and excellence on and off the field, but we rarely embodied a complete team. Instead, we had remained a superstar-oriented franchise since Christy Mathewson roamed the pitcher's mound in the early 20th century. Not even Mays, widely acknowledged as the premier player of his or any era, or Barry Bonds, the all-time home run leader who played 15 seasons for San Francisco, could help us secure baseball's ultimate title.

So when we finally captured the World Series by subduing the Texas Rangers in five games, we were bound to trumpet our achievement as loudly as possible and savor its sweetness as deeply as we could. More than a half-hour of festivities preceding our April 9, 2011, game against the St. Louis Cardinals was dedicated to distributing the rings to the athletic training and coaching staff members, manager Bruce Bochy, and the players.

The rings made a grand entrance into AT&T Park (since renamed Oracle Park). A police escort consisting of nine officers on motorcycles and four on horseback led a procession along the outfield warning track from left to right. Then came the ring bearers, which were borne into the ballpark by a quartet of classic automobiles. Members of the San Francisco Symphony provided musical accompaniment. It was nonstop fanfare.

Considering that the Giants had waited so long for this occasion, nothing was too ostentatious. Broadcaster Duane Kuiper, serving as co-master of ceremonies with on-air partner Mike Krukow, dressed formally in white-tie-and-tails. Kuiper felt compelled to joke to the audience, "Tuxedos, rings—for those of you thinking that Mike and I are going to renew our vows, that's not true."

But who would receive the first ring? There were the executives, who did so much behind the scenes to transform the Giants into winners: Bill Neukom, the club's managing general partner, and Peter Magowan, who led the effort to keep the Giants in San Francisco after the 1992 season when a group of investors reached an agreement in principle to purchase the franchise and move it to Tampa-St. Petersburg. And there was Larry Baer, Magowan's trusted associate, who was at the center of every effort—significant or small—to improve the organization. General manager Brian Sabean, the architect of the championship club, certainly was deserving. So, too, was Bochy, whose persuasive handling of players kept us mentally focused and physically sharp all season.

Each of the rings, which were crafted by Tiffany, sparkled with 77 diamonds, and I had the unbelievable distinction and honor to be the first one of the Giants' inner circle to get his World Series ring. It was humbling. I didn't expect that, but that's the way Larry and Sabes wanted it. I had been here the longest and I always told people I was the bride left at the altar. It made me proud. "It was emotional for Mike and I to announce him as being the first guy," Kuiper said. "We both really wanted to cry."

"He should have been the first," left-hander Barry Zito said. "It's his clubhouse. He sets the tone in that clubhouse. I think a lot of times players start believing this lie that it's all about us all the time. Once a player's gone for the most part, most people forget about that player if you give them enough years. They'll forget that guy's name or if he even existed. Murph has been the slow and steady through all the years in San Francisco. That deserves a huge amount of respect."

Will Clark, the first baseman who was the face of the franchise during most of his 1986–93 tenure with the club, has always represented the franchise with class. He and I are very close. "For 50-something years, Murphy is the heart and soul of the clubhouse," Clark said. "Everything revolved around him—getting your bats ordered, getting your shoes, getting your jerseys and everything, making sure you had food when you came off the field. And Murph would always beat people to the punch. If you slid and tore up your pants—and at Candlestick Park, this used to happen all the time—you'd come back to the dugout,

In a ceremony before the game against the St. Louis Cardinals on April 9, 2011, I march out to the AT&T Park field to receive the first World Series ring. It was one of the great honors of my life. (Getty Images)

and there was Murph standing down there in the tunnel with a new pair of pants if you wanted them. That's just one instance of how he outworked and outthought everybody."

Neukom said the kindest things about me regarding the ring I received. "It's an instinct of service to others. No job is too small," Neukom said. "It's all part of making a group productive. Murph has that instinct. His job explicitly calls for it, but he does it so gracefully and so willingly. He's got people who clean the shoes, but Murph does his share of the shoes. He's got guys who do the laundry, but he does his share of the laundry. That's the range of being the consummate host to Willie Mays to being the guy in the laundry room to being the guy yelled at by Steve Kline—this wonderful banter between two guys with enormous respect for each other."

Citing the "emotional toughness" that was fostered by the likes of Clark, Neukom added, "That culture in the clubhouse can come from veterans, but it also comes from a guy like Murph. Murph would never get rattled. It could be the most shameful end of a game, and he was the same Murph, who's standing there when they came back in the clubhouse, and somebody just hit a walk-off grand slam. He brought that professional notion that there's always going to be another game. He's almost like the great parent who says to his kid, 'How was your game? What did you learn today?' Not 'How many hits did you have? How many assists did you record?' He had that steadying influence. We got more out of the younger, more impressionable players partly because we had the veterans, but I do think to some extent because we had a clubhouse culture led by Murph, which was, 'We're professionals. We're going to learn as we go, we're going to be better-prepared than the other team, and we're going to win games.'"

For years, the assortment of items on my desk in my clubhouse office included a brass plate with the words "character builder" inscribed on it. In that clubhouse everybody could be themselves, wich meant that we had a lot of characters around. Reliever Javier Lopez used to poke fun at my hair. "It was always a little uncombed because you quickly realize that he doesn't sleep a whole lot at night," Lopez said. "He is the last to leave and the first to arrive often at 8:00 AM for a 7:15 PM night game. Last but not least, he always has a key ring attached to his belt loop with what looks like 50 keys on it. You can and still do hear him coming before you see him."

I occasionally enable or even contribute to various players' pranks, such as those that victimized former clubhouse assistant David Loewenstein. Depending on the day of the week, he might get bound, gagged, and deposited in center field; stuffed into a trash receptacle; or wrapped to a medical table by spools of athletic tape. "Murph wasn't the one doing it, but he played along with it and got a few laughs and giggles out of it," Clark said.

I knew Mario Alioto, the Giants' executive vice president of business operations, well because he served as Candlestick Park's visiting team clubhouse manager and as a batboy in his youth. "The difference with Murph is that: over the years when you think about the Giants from a players' standpoint in the environment of the clubhouse, he's the steady piece of this," Alioto said. "A lot of things change. GMs change, and managers change, and players change, but Murph has been here since '58. What does that say about the work he has done and the role he has played? I think it's a bigger role than we give him credit for. When you get behind those doors, you don't quite know what goes on in there. It's this sanctity of the clubhouse, but he's the one who creates that environment. It's a safe zone for the players. That safe zone is Murph's area. That's where he's in charge, and he has created that environment, that safe zone for players, for so long. There is now a trust with him. Through all that he's a friend."

The foremost part of my job is just supplying players with equipment. Reliever Jeremy Affeldt described my role as: "If you need it and I don't have it, I'll figure out a way to get it because I need you to keep your focus on the field and do what you're supposed to do for this team."

Once you're a Giant, you're always a Giant. I've seen every Giants home game since they moved West. I was so honored and humbled when they named our spot in the stadium "the Mike Murphy Clubhouse." "You don't last that long in one place unless you're good at what you do and people like you," shortstop Rich Aurilia said. "All we had to do was walk in and say, 'The best,' and everybody knew you were talking about Murph. He was everybody's grandfather, uncle, brother, dad. He didn't let any of the small stuff get to him. He just went about his business and did his job. At the same time, he respected everybody who was in that clubhouse and in uniform. I can't remember—in my 11 years with him—him ever treating one player differently than another. I think that's what everybody saw in him. He treated everybody the same—whether it was a Hall of Famer or a rookie who just got called up. I always respected that in him because in this game there's a lot of pride, a lot of egos, and a lot of people who get treated different than others, but he was not one of those people who treated people that way. He treated everybody the same. That was what made him different and special."

That's part of what makes the Giants different. Our tradition has remained alive. "It's a lasting brotherhood," said right-hander John D'Acquisto, a Giants player from 1973 to 1976. "Murph's responsible for that. It lives in you until you die."

Krukow, who pitched for two other historic franchises—the Chicago Cubs and Philadelphia Phillies—articulated what being a Giant means. "There's a weight when you put that uniform on," he said. "You can feel 125 years. You really can. I think that there's a responsibility. You're not just a player. You're a curator. The people who played before you established this franchise. You're keenly aware of that history when you put that uniform on for the first time and you're keenly aware of the rivalry you have with the Dodgers. So I think that there's a responsibility with this club that a lot of teams don't have. When you win here, there's such a deep feeling of respect from the fans that lasts well beyond the last game played that season. They don't forget you, and that's a humbling thing for an athlete."

I still like to stay busy in the clubhouse: "He's not there full time, but where is he every day? I guarantee you at some point today, he's at that clubhouse with his dog, hanging out doing something, walking to Red's Java House for lunch," Aurilia said in March of 2019. "It's what he knows and who he is, and he'll never change. The game will never see anybody else like that."

That's nice of Aurilia to say, but the clubhouse belongs to the players. And gone are the days when ballplayers lingered at the ballpark after a game for a couple of hours, maybe longer.

They'd unwind with a cigarette or two, a beverage or two, and maybe start a game of cards. But they also dissected the game they just played. They had no Twitter or Facebook giving them opportunities to express their thoughts on social media. If they had children at home to take care of, their wives did it. Aurilia reached the big leagues when this era had virtually ended. "We used to call it 'Club Murph.'" Aurilia said. "It would always be the veteran guys after a game, when everybody else was gone and we're still sitting there, hanging out, having a beer. Murph would put on Sinatra and he'd be vacuuming and singing with a cigar in his mouth. He would not leave until the last player left that clubhouse. That shows what a true professional he was and the level of respect he had for us, which in turn gave us the love and the level of respect we had for him."

My boss with the Giants, Eddie Logan, set a standard for conduct around players that guided me through my early years: "Be on time, never borrow money from a ballplayer, and if you need something, I'll get it for you. If you need money, I'll give it to you."

I'm lucky to have served as an example to other clubbies. "I think you have to take a look at his tenure and how much time he's put in," Colorado Rockies clubhouse manager Mike Pontarelli said. "We all know throughout Major League Baseball how hard we all grind and how many days we're working and hours we put in. To sustain that for as many years as Murph was able to endure it and really just kind of grind through all the years and do it with a smile on his face—I never saw him in a bad mood—that's difficult to do. So to set that kind of example for the rest of clubhouse guys, I have all the respect in the world for Murph."

Like Pontarelli, our kind tends to stick around. Pete Sheehy ran the New York Yankees' clubhouse and held related posts for the staggering span of 1927 to 1985. Sheehy became a legend because that's what happens to people who are associated with the Yankees that long and because he was great at what he did. Yosh Kawano, who died in 2018 at age 97, spent 65 years working both clubhouses at various times for the Cubs. No wonder he was dubbed "the king of Wrigley Field." I tried to be as dependable as those great men. "If you wanted anything done, you went to Murph," right-hander Bob Bolin said. "The last 40 years, Murph handled everything. You could always depend on him. If you needed something and he said he'd do it, he'd always do it."

Lon Simmons, the hugely popular voice of the Giants and 49ers who was inducted into the broadcasters' wing of the Hall of Fame after winning the Ford C. Frick award in 2004, remembers a time of happy mayhem. The date was September 30, 1971, and we had just clinched the National League West title by defeating the San Diego Padres on the road 5–1. We'd win the playoff opener two days later, when the Giants edged the Pittsburgh Pirates 5–4, but this was the last classic victory in the franchise's Bay Area history. Mays drove in a key run with an RBI double off the center-field wall. McCovey added a pair of hits. Marichal pitched a complete-game five-hitter. Fans far and wide listened to the festivities on the Giants' radio network and yearned to hear their heroes' voices after they had fended off the rival Los Angeles Dodgers for the division championship.

The problem with these celebrations is that people tend to vanish. Players usually aren't at their dressing stalls, as is the case in most postgame settings. Instead, players vanish amid cascades of beer and champagne. They often seek an abandoned storage room or some other private place to express their joy in solitude. But that night, Simmons' broadcast partner, Bill Thompson, managed to get just about every Giants hero on the air with my assistance. I was happy to help, and it's also my duty to help. "Those clubhouse managers take care of you. That's their job," Aurilia said. "I'd say the difference [with Murphy] is on the personal level—the amount of caring and compassion and love, whatever you want to call it, that he had for his players. If somebody had a problem with Murph, well then, they need to look in the mirror because the problem is probably with themselves. It's not with Murph."

"I don't think he plays any favorites among the players," Neukom said. "I know he's got favorites; don't we all. It's human nature. But I think he treats that rookie just like he treats the Hall of Famers-to-be."

I certainly root for the Giants, but my 19 years spent managing the visitors' clubhouse taught me some great guys wear uniforms other than San Francisco's. I became chummy with players like Don Drysdale, Stan Musial, Bob Uecker, Joe Torre, and Willie Stargell. "He's very, very accommodating," Alioto said. "He'd be a perfect concierge at the best hotel in the world. But he does it with a smile. It pleases him to please others. And the thing about Murph is he's so comfortable with who he is and what his role is."

I can recall with amusement the errands that Torre sent me on during the mornings of getaway days, the series-ending games that are scheduled for afternoons to facilitate travel. When managing the Atlanta Braves and St. Louis Cardinals, Torre requested food items that could easily be obtained in San Francisco but were difficult to find elsewhere: frozen ravioli, certain wines and cheeses, and focaccia bread. I'm glad he never sent me up to the wine country. Torre was a great guy, and I'd do anything for him. Just like I'd do anything for any of my managers.

He, of course, won four World Series rings. I am so fortunate and honored to get that first one with the Giants. That was so unexpected and humbling. "That was awesome," Clark said. "Of all people, he should have been the one to get it first—by far. You look at the Willie Mayses and the Willie McCoveys and the Gaylords and the Marichals and then you look at Jack Clark and then my era and Barry Bonds' era. He made it through all of that and he made it all happen behind the scenes. You have assistants and stuff like that, but he damn near did it by himself."

Before we continue, here's a note to the uninitiated: in baseball the place where players, coaches, and the manager gather before, during, and after performing their jobs each day is called a clubhouse. It is *not* a locker room. "A locker room is just a place to go get dressed, and there are a thousand of them," Clark said. "A clubhouse is like a big family. When all of those pieces work really well—the term for it is 'chemistry'—it's really easy to go out there on the field and do your job."

"A locker room is where you get dressed and cleaned up," Neukom said. "A clubhouse has so much more going on in terms of sociology. People spend real time there. It's not a point of transit. It's a point of experience and expression. If your clubhouse is well-organized and well-managed, you have a heck of an advantage, and it shows, and that falls to the clubhouse manager."

Ask Dave Righetti. The Giants' longtime pitching coach (2000–17) spent most of his active playing career with the Yankees. With legends such as Mickey Mantle, Yogi Berra, and Whitey Ford liable to materialize on any given day, being a Yankee meant knowing that clubhouse is indeed a compound word. It's the ballclub's house, its home. And who lives in houses and homes? Families. "A locker room sounds like someplace where you hang your clothes. A clubhouse is a place where you can be yourself," Righetti said. "To me, it used to be sacred ground."

Mays, who I befriended almost immediately during the Giants' 1958 inaugural season in San Francisco, echoed Righetti's sentiment: "The clubhouse man is very sacred."

From Seals Stadium to Candlestick Park to Oracle Park, I loved working in that sacred clubhouse—even if it included some gritty tasks. "I mean, the guy frickin' cleans shoes," Zito said. "I know that everyone you talk to is going to say that, but the first thing that anyone ever wants to stop doing as a clubhouse worker is probably clean shoes. And Murph still cleans shoes. He's not just sitting back at his desk, bossing people around. He's in there doing it. I mean, Murph needs to write a book on life lessons."

Sure, there are mundane tasks. But I've always said: if you love your job, you don't work a day in your life.

"First of all, Murph loves the game," Alioto said. "But he started out with the job he wanted to end at. It's not like he's doing this to get to the next level. He's a baseball guy who understands the behind-the-scenes part of his business. To this day, I believe there's a trust they have in Murph that, whatever the issue is—something about the team, something with his personal life—Murph is involved. And I think that means a lot to a lot of these guys because the business is such a public business that sometimes you have to let your hair down with somebody. And I think Murph is that person. Sounding board, confessional, he played a different role for a lot of guys."

Alioto was linked to the Giants more than most kids. His brother, Carl, was the visiting team's batboy at Candlestick Park. Mario accompanied their father on his route for the Atlas Linen Company, delivering clean towels to and picking up soiled ones from the clubhouses. That experience was enough to rouse the younger son's curiosity about the mystique of the clubhouse. "I remember just the smell of the clubhouse to this day—the rubbing alcohol, the pine tar," Mario Alioto said. "It's weird, but I still remember that as if it were yesterday."

After one game I had a particularly large mess to clean and asked the Aliotos to lend a hand. "I helped Murph for two minutes, sweeping up something and helping with the dustpan," Alioto said. "He gave me $5 and said, 'Go get yourself some cold cuts.'"

Halfway through the 1973 season, Carl realized that he couldn't free himself for every Giants' home date. This created the opportunity for Mario, who had proven to me that he would work diligently for a slice or two of bologna, to inherit Carl's duties. "It was odd for me to wear the visiting uniform all the time, but I loved it," Mario Alioto said, "except for the Dodgers' one. I never thought I would get booed when I was 12."

Each team, it seemed, had its resident legends and distinct personalities. "I think back quite often on who the players were at that time in that era who went through that clubhouse," Alioto said. "From Hank Aaron and Manny Sanguillen and Johnny Bench and Pete Rose and Bob Gibson and Gaylord [Perry] when he played for the Padres, name a team, and I can probably name you all the guys on that team. Every team was different. The Dodgers had more people in the clubhouse, I think, because they were [geographically] closer. The Pirates, back in the '70s with 'We Are Family,' oh, they were messy and they were loud. I remember one time in August—I can't remember what year it was—they came in from L.A. and had just taken over first place. It was like a party in there. The stereo was blasting all different kinds of music. But you could tell they were close. The Cincinnati Reds and the Mets always came in blazers. The Cardinals dressed casually and wore jeans."

Since Alioto and his counterparts didn't get paid much—$7 per game, $10 for doubleheaders—the least I could do was take the batboys and the clubhouse staff out for breakfast on Saturdays and Sundays at DiRocca's on Mission Street. "He was like your grandfather," Alioto said. "He picked up everything. Whether we were 12, 13, 14, 15, or 16 years old, he made us feel like big leaguers. That was Murph."

One day one of the other batboys told me, "I can't work this weekend. It's my high school prom." So I tossed him a set of keys and said, "Take my car. You'll look better." I was driving a Lincoln Continental at the time.

This idyllic life ended, or so Alioto thought, when he quit the Giants after the 1978 season to attend college at St. Mary's. Back at Candlestick Park, big changes were developing behind the scenes. Logan, the team's clubhouse manager since 1947—after beginning as an assistant in 1933—decided to retire after the 1979 season. I became the Giants' clubhouse manager in 1980, and "Sweet" Lou Brinson took over the visitors' clubhouse. Then Brinson perished in an automobile accident in February, shortly before spring training began.

The Giants needed somebody knowledgeable, and they needed him quickly. That's how Alioto ended up running the visitors' clubhouse from 1980 to 1982. He did such a great job for us, and I've really enjoyed working with him. "He's the best at deflecting any attention," Alioto said. "I've seen him a couple of times when he's been honored. 'Aaaah, I've got nuthin' to say.' Because in the clubhouse, you're the person behind the curtain. In a way that's how he has kind of rubbed off on me a little bit. Because in this business, it's not about us. It's about what's happening on the field. But I think in recent years, he has come to understand a little bit that in a way it's a little bit about him. He's been part of the show probably more so than he's willing to give himself credit for."

I'm about the same age as Bolin, but I'm friends with players of all ages and levels of acclaim. The greatest of them all, Mays, is a bit cautious with strangers, and McCovey often wore a quiet, reserved exterior and needed decades of nurturing. "How does that friendship develop over time? It has to be based on trust," Alioto said.

I felt fortunate to share that kind of trust with the 1989 team that won the National League pennant. Kevin Mitchell, the left fielder who had such a great year and won the league's MVP award, said the kindest things to say about me. "He was our MVP," Mitchell said. "He should be in the Hall of Fame."

On that same '89 team was Matt Williams, the enormously popular slugging third baseman who thrived with the Giants from 1987 to 1996. I really enjoyed spending time with him in

Ring Ceremony

I hang out with the clubhouse crew in Scottsdale, Arizona, after becoming clubhouse manager in 1980. (Mike Murphy)

the clubhouse. "Murph is quite an amazing story," Williams said. "It's a story of longevity and love for the game. Among other things in his life, the constant has always been the Giants. His feelings for the organization and for all the teams that he has seen come through is deep, and he's still there today. Although his role is not as great as it once was, he's still there. He loves it. I imagine he'd be so bored if he didn't go to the ballpark. He always makes sure he comes and says hello. He treated me just like he treated anybody else, made sure I had everything I needed, made sure that he welcomed me to the Giants. Your first impressions of people are important because I was really wet behind the ears, and he took me in and showed me how to do it. His job was to make sure that we were able to not worry about anything else but going out there and playing the game. He's a master at that."

Right-hander Ryan Vogelsong was a master of his craft and quite a find. Drafted by the Giants in the fifth round in 1998, Vogelsong was traded to Pittsburgh and spent the better part of a decade struggling with the Pirates, their farm system, and in Japanese baseball. He returned to the Giants as a non-roster invitee to spring training in 2011 and briefly went to Triple A before being summoned to replace an injured Zito in the starting rotation. Three months later Vogelsong was named to the National League All-Star team and was the Giants' leading winner in the 2012 postseason.

It meant a lot to hear Vogelsong discuss my role when he received his first big league experience in 2001. "'Hey, kiddo, I don't know if you should be doing that.' That's what Murph was for me," Vogelsong said. "He taught me things that the other guys kind of forgot about or missed. As much as the guys taught me how to be a pro, Murph taught me more about how to be a pro—when to be quiet, when you speak up, don't be the last one out of the clubhouse before the game starts. Murph's seen a lot, man. Murph's seen it all. Even though he's not a manager or a coach, he's pretty close."

The Giants recalled Vogelsong in 2011. "They treated me like I had 10 years in the big leagues when I hadn't been there for two days," Vogelsong said. "A lot of that was because I did things the right way. And the only way I knew how to do things the right way was because I had Murph watching my back. What he did for me when I was 23, I'll never forget it."

He hasn't. After spending 2011–15 with the Giants, Vogelsong signed with the Pirates as a free agent. When Pittsburgh visited San Francisco, he always reserved 20 minutes for a pregame chat with me, which wasn't necessary at all. My philosophy always has been: I don't bother nobody. I don't want to get too involved in somebody's business. I want to make sure they have space. "When you're together so much with all these guys, so many little tiny things can—not set guys off—but kind of grate on people, put you on edge," Righetti said. "It doesn't matter how the clubhouse is going. There's always somebody upset; there's somebody overly too happy. You need certain kinds of people around to keep everything on an even keel because they've seen it all. And he was that guy. I've seen him mad but very rarely. I think that's why he's loved so much.

"What a perfect demeanor to do that job. You weren't afraid to ask for something because he wasn't going to make fun of you and embarrass you in front of the players. That's a big thing because clubhouse guys have a tendency to 'work' guys, depending on who's tipping him the most. But Murph didn't deal in that. In fact, he wouldn't even give me a bill. I said, 'Murph, you gotta give me a bill so I can pay you properly.' He'd say, 'Aaaah, just give me what you want.' I'd say, 'How are you going to take the missus to Reno for bingo?' We had to force him to do that. We knew they were under pressure in that clubhouse because he had to pay for the food in that clubhouse. Everything the players got, he had to pay for. And he had to deal with our front office. So we didn't ever want to put him in a bad position. So you took care of Murph because you knew he'd take care of you. So the best part of coming to the Giants might have been Murph for me, and I mean that wholeheartedly because that's where you lived every day."

2

Willie Mays

NOT MUCH HAS CHANGED in my relationship with Willie Mays through the decades. Except that I love him more every year. We've been there for each other because, well, we have to be! There aren't a lot of guys left from that original San Francisco Giants team of 1958. Johnny Antonelli, an excellent left-handed starter, is still going strong. But we don't see much of him because he lives near Rochester, New York. Orlando Cepeda, though, still gets to the ballpark quite often.

Sadly, we lost Willie McCovey in the fall of 2018. Jimmy Davenport died in 2016. I think about those guys all the time. Not only were they great friends of mine, but they also took so much pride in being Giants. The instant Willie Mac was traded to the San Diego Padres in the 1973 offseason, he wanted to come back to San Francisco. It's great that we give the Willie McCovey award to the team's most inspirational player every year. And, of course, McCovey Cove sits out beyond right field at the ballpark. I've met people who can't name the ballpark, but they know what McCovey Cove is. That guarantees that McCovey's name will carry on.

Davenport was so faithful that he stayed with the Giants, even though they fired him before he could finish his one and only season as manager in 1985. Oh, he spent a couple of years with a couple of other organizations, but in his heart, he never stopped being a Giant. He spent his last several years as a roving instructor and scout for the Giants, and I thought it was the greatest thing that the regulars of the last homegrown infield the team had—first baseman Brandon Belt, second baseman Joe Panik, shortstop Brandon Crawford, and third baseman Matt Duffy—each gave Davvy a lot of credit for helping their development.

As for Mays, I still get as much of a kick out of him as I ever did. He drops by the clubhouse probably once or twice a homestand. We talk a lot, but it's not just reminiscing about all those great times we had with the old Giants. We might talk about the current ballclub, the state of baseball—once you get Willie started talking about baseball, it's hard to get him to stop—or we'll discuss the kind of stuff that any pair of old friends might talk about like family or mutual interests. As Mays likes to say, "Just talk."

He will turn 89 years old in 2020. Almost everybody who has lived that long has experienced some physical challenges, and he's no exception. His superior vision during his professional heyday enabled him to distinguish a fastball from a curveball more quickly than anybody could. But for the last few years, cataracts have virtually blinded him. His base-running ability once bedeviled opponents and captivated fans. Now he tries to stay off his feet a lot, so he rides in a golf cart when it's practical. He has heard more cheering than almost any human being on this planet during his years on this Earth. He can still hear the cheering as long as he keeps his hearing aids properly tuned and battery-powered.

Naturally, it's tough to watch somebody you adore grow older. But Mays makes things better just by being himself. He can be a little grouchy at times. But he has earned the right. To this day, I get a thrill from watching him come through those clubhouse doors. Our friendship was never based on hero worship. It's always been based on trust.

It's funny, but before the Giants came West, I didn't know much about him. Certainly, I had heard of him and knew that he was a fantastic center fielder. But partly because the Seals were a Boston Red Sox affiliate, Ted Williams was my first favorite ballplayer. Once the '58 season started, it quickly became obvious Mays wasn't just the Giants' best player. He was the planet's best player. I didn't have time to help him with any special favors given how busy I was. And you know what? Mays noticed that and appreciated it.

Pretty soon, he and I became confidants. Lord knows, Mays needed friends. Despite having one of his best seasons—the .347 batting average he recorded that season was a personal best— he struggled to win over the San Francisco fans. Even the local newspapers took sides. *The San Francisco News* tended to be harsh on Mays mainly because another paper, *The Call-Bulletin*, signed him up to do a ghostwritten column. Purists dismissed Mays by insisting that Joe DiMaggio, a San Francisco native, was a better ballplayer. Newcomers to baseball—and there were many of them due to the novelty of the Giants—preferred Cepeda, the home-grown first baseman. Cepeda had a great year (.312 batting average, 25 home runs, 96 RBIs) and won the National League Rookie of the Year award. But he was no Mays, who lost the league's batting title by .003 to Philadelphia Phillies star Richie Ashburn.

Nowhere was Mays taken for granted or just flat-out spurned more than he was in the National League Most Valuable Player balloting. For example, in 1958, Mays' first season in San Francisco, he finished second in the MVP voting to Ernie Banks. The Chicago Cubs slugger amassed 47 homers and 129 RBIs compared to Willie's 29 and 96. Yet Mays was more productive overall, leading the league in runs scored, stolen bases, and OPS (on-base plus slugging percentage).

Even worse was 1960, when voters seemed bent on giving the award to anybody who played for the pennant-winning Pittsburgh Pirates. Mays didn't top the non-Pirates contingent, finishing third behind winner Dick Groat and Don Hoak. Mays rapped a league-high 190 hits that year, but only 29 were homers largely because that was the Giants' first season in Candlestick Park, where the dimensions (420 feet to center field and 390 to the left-field power alley) conspired to limit Mays to 12 round-trippers at home. The lunacy of the voting is best explained by employing more contemporary logic. Mays had a league-best 9.5 WAR, a statistic that wasn't even dreamed of in 1960. It meant that he contributed at a rate that would have produced nine-and-a-half more victories than a team of replacement-level players. The WAR figures for Groat and Hoak were 6.2 and 5.4, respectively. Bottom line: Mays should have won more MVP awards than the ones he collected in 1954 and 1965.

Mays and I rarely discussed such topics when we had our dugout chats. One subject Mays focused on, however, was my financial well-being. Mays was aware that we batboys and clubbies made very little money and he intended to guarantee that I avoided any financial hardship. "I wanted to make sure that he understood that if he didn't have enough money to buy a suit or a pair of pants," Mays said, "I'll take care of it. But I didn't tell everybody about it."

During the glimpses of game action that I was able to catch, I saw Mays do things nobody else could, especially on defense. Vin Scully, the great Dodgers broadcaster, summed it up best when he said that Mays played center field as if he were a shortstop, charging batted balls and coming up throwing. "You had to because we had some great runners in my time," Mays said.

The other thing Mays did was play shallow in center, daring opponents to smack drives over his head. This often did them more harm than good. I asked him if he did this only at Seals Stadium, which had a relatively small outfield. "I played shallow everywhere because I figured if he hits it in the air, I could catch it. That's the way I played. If the guy that's hitting sees me playing shallow, he's going to try to hit it over my head. And that's how I got them out a lot because they hit it high and I could catch it without any problem."

Just like the love of the game clause in Michael Jordan's first professional contract that allowed him to participate in offseason pickup games, Mays needed something like that in his contract. There were times he wouldn't leave Seals Stadium for three or four hours after the game ended because he'd play makeshift games with us batboys. He'd bat left-handed because if he had hit righty he couldn't help but hit it out of the park. I played first base. "Doc" Hughes was the catcher. It was far from a real game since we never played nine-on-nine. But it was a heck of a lot of fun to play something resembling baseball with the best player in the world.

My fellow San Franciscans were still mostly unmoved. After Russian premier Nikita Khrushchev basked in a friendly reception during a 1959 visit to San Francisco, journalist Frank Coniff observed, "San Fransisco is the damnedest city I ever saw in my life. They cheer Khrushchev and boo Willie Mays."

If any of that stuff bothered Mays, he never showed it. He kept swinging as if his bat were an axe that would chop down the skepticism that loomed over him. His gargantuan home run on the final day of the 1962 regular season that helped send the Giants into a best-of-three playoff with the Los Angeles Dodgers for the National League pennant won him some believers.

My friend, Willie Mays, and I hang out in the clubhouse. (Mike Murphy)

May 4, 1966, was one of the best nights ever. In that game Mays hit his 512th career home run off Claude Osteen of the Dodgers to pass Mel Ott and become No. 1 on the National League's all-time home run list. League records were a much bigger deal then compared to now. Various factors, most notably interleague play, have blurred the lines between the leagues. But at this time, this accomplishment of Mays apparently impressed even the usual skeptics. He received a prolonged ovation from the fans that seemed to be a legitimate gesture of acceptance. From then on, I remember mostly hearing cheers for Mays.

The cheering stopped in May of 1972, when the Giants did the unthinkable and traded Mays to the New York Mets. This trade wasn't made for the usual reasons. Giants owner Horace Stoneham was losing money at a dangerously high rate and didn't want Mays to be present for what almost was the demise of the franchise. Joan Payson, the Mets' principal owner, promised to take care of Mays financially after his playing days ended—just as Mr. Stoneham wanted to do himself. Though this was a move meant to benefit Willie in the long run, it was the worst day of my life.

Gone was his reassuring presence that to me could mean anything from fatherly advice to a high-pitched squeal of laughter over some silly joke. Just the mere sight of him reminded all of us that we were the Giants, which by itself was a source of pride. A lot of people thought Mays would be happy to finish his major league career in New York, the city where it began. A lot of people were wrong. "I didn't want to go there," Mays said. "I had all my friends out here. I got to know a lot of people out here—on the Avenues, on the team. The owners were good to me, but Mrs. Payson was good to me. She said, 'Anything you want here, we're gonna get it for you.'"

Of course, I visited Mays whenever I could. Years after the trade, somebody asked Mays whether he missed me as much as I missed him. "No," Mays said. "Murph always found me."

I always was mindful of the many, many tasks I had to handle when Mays came in and I was still head clubhouse manager. But I did make sure that Mays was taken care of quickly. I would have at least a bowl of soup and a plate of crackers ready for him as soon as he settled in his chair. Nowadays, the Giants employ professional chefs to ease the players' shared obligation to maintain a proper diet. For years I brought soup, salad, and sandwiches to Mays. Now the Giants' chefs offer him specials such as ahi tuna, as if he were dining at one of San Francisco's finest restaurants. That's the way they treat ballplayers nowadays.

Nothing has changed the bond that Mays and I share. Though I lost my big, main office when the clubhouse was remodeled and I entered semi-retirement in 2015, two of the items hanging on the walls of my new office are photographs of me and Mays. One photo features Mays in a full Giants uniform and was shot in 2018 on the day he videotaped a Toyota commercial with Buster Posey.

People used to say, "You never know who you'll see in Murph's office." That's still true today. Late in the 2019 season, for instance, Joe Torre, who handles disciplinary matters for the commissioner's office, dropped by Oracle Park to congratulate Giants manager Bruce Bochy on his retirement. Like many baseball veterans and lifers, Torre and I go way back—all the way back to 1961, when I ran the visitors' clubhouse at Candlestick Park and he broke into the majors as a rookie catcher with the Milwaukee Braves. Mays happened to be there too, which prompted a few extra laughs.

Before Torre arrived, we reminisced about some of the commercials and endorsements that came Mays' way. He did one for Coca-Cola, in which I stood at first. I earned $1,000. Not bad for a day of standing around! Mays also endorsed Chesterfield cigarettes, even though he doesn't smoke, and Coors beer, even though he doesn't drink a drop. A little-known ad, mainly because it was regional, was one he did for Alaga pancake syrup. This one was more fitting because Mays came from Alabama, and Alaga is a combination of the abbreviations of Alabama and Georgia.

Somehow, Mays' assistant managed to find a videotape of a TV commercial that he did with Mickey Mantle for Blue Bonnet Margarine. Mays laughed at the memory of taping what should have been a fairly simple ad. "It took us all day to do it because we couldn't sing," said Mays before breaking into an off-key rendition of the product's jingle of "Everything's better with Blue Bonnet on it." Summing up the TV shoot, Mays said, "We didn't know what the hell we were doing."

At about that time, Torre entered my office, having exchanged pleasantries with Bochy. Aware of Mays' poor hearing, Torre spoke at a relatively high volume: "Willie Mays! Joe Torre! How are you, Willie?"

Mays uttered a profanity—not at all out of malice, just as a way of saying, "Here it comes."

Torre didn't miss a beat. "That's the Willie Mays I know and love," he said.

We quickly began talking about Bob Gibson, the legendary St. Louis Cardinals right-hander who announced during the summer of 2019 that he had been diagnosed with cancer. Torre and Mays compared notes on telephone conversations they recently had with Gibson. Reminiscing soon followed. Torre brought up an occasion when first baseman Bill White, who was traded from the Giants to the Cardinals, visited Mays' home in San Francisco for a postgame meal. Gibson, who was just beginning to establish his reputation as baseball's chief badass, accompanied White. Gibson sported the spectacles that he typically wore off the field. Mays was mortified to learn that such a hard thrower as Gibson needed glasses. No wonder Mays' career batting average against Gibson was so modest. Mays asked Gibson at dinner, "Are you crazy? As hard as you throw and knock me down, you gotta wear something [on the field], man."

Mays even recalled a game when he simply did not want to step in the batter's box against Gibson. "[Umpire] Shag Crawford asked me one day, 'Are you going to hit?'" When Mays said no, Crawford warned that he'd call him out. "Shoot, I'll go sit down," Mays joked.

I reminded them that Gibson broke Jim Ray Hart's shoulder—not once but twice. That's how Gibson dealt with opposing hitters who took big, carefree swings against him. Mays said that he advised Hart to be ready to avoid Gibson's wicked knockdown pitches: "I told him, 'When you swing hard, you gotta be able to go on the ground.' He swung, and on the next pitch, Gibby hit him on the shoulder. I said, 'You couldn't show up Gibby, I can tell you one thing because he'll always remember you. He'll get you somewhere along the line.' He was nice as pie, though, when he wasn't pitching."

Mays' presence stirred Torre's memory banks. "He was always relaxed as any hitter I've ever known," said Torre, who resorted to unusual means to try to break his concentration. "The first thing

I would do is not put a sign down," Torre said. "He says, 'I know what you're doing.' I figured: let him wait. There was one time I asked him a question, and as he was answering the question, he hit a home run. Willie said, 'I'll talk to you when I get back.'"

I was in and out of the office because I had to help the clubhouse staff prepare for that night's game against the Colorado Rockies, Finally, I ducked into my office to relax with his guests for a few minutes. "I miss you, Murph," Torre blurted out at one point.

"I'm still here," I said.

The 1960s

I never doubted the Giants. Many times, though, they left me scratching my head. Those 1960s teams had so much talent. Yet they won only one National League pennant and they had to edge the Los Angeles Dodgers in a best-of-three playoff to earn that triumph.

I remember seeing a copy of the *San Francisco Chronicle* one day in the mid-1960s. I grabbed it and, of course, went straight to "The Sporting Green." It was either their spring training or regular-season special preview section. I'm not sure which. Anyway, here's my point: On the section's front page was this huge photo of Willie Mays, Willie McCovey, Orlando Cepeda, and Jim Ray Hart standing shoulder to shoulder. Imagine unleashing that kind of offensive firepower upon the rest of the league. However, that particular foursome rarely thrived together. McCovey batted .220 in 1964, and Cepeda rarely played in 1965 due to a knee injury before being traded to the St. Louis Cardinals early in the '66 season.

We didn't know it then, but the Giants' fate was sealed for the 1960s when McCovey's line drive traveled directly to New York Yankees second baseman Bobby Richardson, sending San Francisco to a 1–0 loss in Game 7 of the 1962 World Series. Had McCovey's smash eluded Richardson for a hit, Mays and Matty Alou would have scored to win the Fall Classic for the Giants. And who knows how the rest of the decade would have unfolded?

We, of course, now know what happened. The Giants finished second in the National League for five consecutive seasons from 1965 to 1969. This set in motion a chain of events that almost ended the franchise's stay in San Francisco. Tired of close but no cigar, the fanbase dwindled, and attendance dropped. The arrival of the Oakland A's in 1968 particularly cut into the Giants' attendance, which dipped below a million annually after hovering around 1.5 million since the move to Candlestick Park in 1960. Management couldn't or wouldn't market its stars. Priorities changed. Younger adults were much more concerned with the Vietnam War and social changes than the pennant race. By the mid-1970s, the Giants were largely considered irrelevant. Their season attendance dipped to barely more than 500,000, and they damn near moved to Toronto before the 1976 season.

Of course, the Giants envisioned none of this. They simply kept trying gallantly and fruitlessly. Several players from that era recalled the heartache in a 2008 interview. McCovey, who referred to Game 7 of the '62 World Series as "the day I hit the line drive," summarized the Giants' confidence: "When we lost to the Yankees in 1962, we thought, *Heck, we were going to be back again for the next 10 years*. That's why it didn't bother us so much to lose that

World Series because, hey, we have a good enough team. We'll be back. Little did I know that we would never be back."

The Giants remained a formidable ballclub for the remainder of the decade, though they didn't reach the World Series again until 1989. Following 1962, they won 90 games or more in five of the next seven seasons and 88 in the two others. But the Los Angeles Dodgers, who won three National League pennants in that span, and the Cardinals, National League champions in 1967–68, ultimately outclassed the Giants.

The introduction of divisional play in 1969 was expected to help the Giants. No longer would the Cardinals concern them. But they again placed second, finishing three games behind the Atlanta Braves in the National League West.

Through that period, four of baseball's greatest players sustained the Giants: Mays, McCovey, and right-handers Juan Marichal and Gaylord Perry. Mays became the second player to hit 600 home runs and the first to steal 300 bases and hit that many homers. From 1965 to 1970, McCovey hit .291 and averaged 38 homers and 106 RBIs per season. He and Hank Aaron led all big leaguers with 226 homers apiece in this span. McCovey stood alone at the top with 636 RBIs. Marichal won 191 games in the 1960s, more than any other pitcher. But this impressive cast couldn't compensate for the team's inability to execute the game's subtleties as well as the Dodgers and Cardinals could.

Near Misses

Before the Giants won their 2010 championship, I endured several years when the Giants contended for a title or even reached the World Series but met with frustration each time. This prompted me to compare myself to a "bride left at the altar." Here's how jilted I felt about San Francisco's most notable near misses in the postseason.

1959

The Giants were feeling good about themselves on the night of September 17. Jack Sanford defeated Milwaukee Braves ace Warren Spahn in a 13–6 decision that gave the first-place Giants a two-game lead in the National League standings over the Braves and Los Angeles Dodgers with eight to play. I thought we were going to win it, for sure. I fell asleep on so many nights, imagining the thrill of being the Giants' batboy for the first World Series in San Francisco history.

Two days later, the Giants experienced what must still be considered one of the most disastrous days in their San Francisco history. They dropped a day/night doubleheader to the Dodgers at Seals Stadium 4–1 and 5–3. Los Angeles won Sunday's series finale. That left the Giants and Dodgers tied with Milwaukee a half-game back. The Giants departed on a season-ending trip to Chicago and St. Louis. Back-to-back walk-off losses to the Cubs at Wrigley Field essentially ended our pennant race.

1962

Records show, and history reminds us that the New York Yankees defeated the Giants four games to three in a dramatic World Series. But I know what really beat us that October: the rain. Showers halted play for three days between Games 5 and 6. Though the storms affected both teams, the Yankees were accustomed to dealing with postseason distractions. The Giants weren't. We couldn't get it back into action. I tried, though.

Billy Pierce, the Giants' scheduled starter for Game 6, was in jeopardy of missing his between-starts throwing session because the rain had left the bullpen mounds at Candlestick Park in such poor shape. But Pierce reasoned that the groundskeepers' huge equipment shed located beneath the grandstand down the right-field line afforded him enough room to play catch and at least keep his arm limber. However, none of the Giants' catchers—Ed Bailey, Tom Haller, or John Orsino—was on the scene. So, drawing upon my catching experience in various youth leagues, I volunteered to take Pierce's throws. I yelled to Pierce, "Don't throw the ball too hard. I don't have a mask."

I had nothing to worry about. Pierce had the right touch all year, whether he was playing catch with me or staring down Frank Robinson or Roberto Clemente. He won all 12 of his regular-season starts at Candlestick that year. And when Game 6 was finally played, he tamed the Yankees 5–2 with a complete-game, three-hitter.

I was in the Yankees' clubhouse when Willie McCovey lined out to second baseman Bobby Richardson with two runners aboard to end the World Series. You could hear the crowd react to the batted ball, but there wasn't much of a sound after Richardson caught it.

1965

This season launched the Giants' infamous streak of five consecutive second-place finishes. How this particular team managed to avoid winning the pennant, I'll never know.

It wasn't as if we choked or wilted under pressure. The Giants finished 21–9 in September, including a 14-game winning streak from September 4–16. At the end of this streak, they led the Los Angeles Dodgers and Cincinnati Reds by four-and-a-half games.

But it was like a pro football team taking the lead in the fourth quarter and leaving just a little too much time on the clock for a quarterback like Johnny Unitas, Joe Montana, or Tom Brady. They always found a way to beat you. And our nemesis was always the Dodgers. Those suckers won 13 in a row from September 16–30. They did it in classic Dodgers fashion, too: only three times in that stretch did they allow more than one run in a game. Their pitching was remarkable.

1966

This began as a slow-motion free-fall and ended up as a mad scramble. The Giants dropped out of a first-place tie with the Pittsburgh Pirates on September 2. They remained on the fringes of the pennant race from then on yet didn't sustain even a small winning streak that would have tightened up the standings. From September 2–20 they lurched to a 7–11 record and trailed the first-place Los Angeles Dodgers by five games at the end of this period. Then on September 21, the Giants avoided a four-game series sweep at home against Pittsburgh when Juan Marichal, of all people, lined a tiebreaking, ninth-inning home run that sealed a 6–5 victory. We were stunned by the victory. It gave us some momentum for a three-city, eight-game trip, during which we'd pretty much have to run the table just to have a remote chance at catching the first-place Dodgers.

And that's basically what we did. After splitting a two-game series at the Houston Astros, we won three in a row at the Atlanta Braves. Then after a Friday rainout at Pittsburgh, we swept a Saturday doubleheader, which left us two games behind the Dodgers. If we won our game and if the Philadelphia Phillies could have somehow swept the Dodgers, we'd have been a half-game back and would have had to play a rained-out game to determine the top of the National League standings.

We did our part by beating the Pirates 7–3 in 11 innings. But those damned Dodgers teased us. They lost the first game of their doubleheader 4–3 and then sent Sandy Koufax out to pitch on two days' rest. As usual, Koufax was Koufax. He shut out Philadelphia for eight innings, finished with a complete-game seven-hitter, walked one, and struck out 10. The Dodgers went to the World Series, and we went home.

1969

When divisional play began, a lot of so-called experts believed that this format guaranteed the Giants a postseason spot. We finished second in the National League during the previous two seasons to the St. Louis Cardinals, who were being assigned to the NL East division. Our archrivals, the Los Angeles Dodgers, joined us in the NL West, but they were still recovering from Sandy Koufax's retirement following the 1966 season. And nobody yet knew that early in '69 Don Drysdale would quit playing, too. So our chief competitors for the division title appeared to be the Cincinnati Reds, who had assembled one hell of a lineup, and the Atlanta Braves, who had some decent pitching, as well as Hank Aaron at the top of his game. The Houston Astros appeared to have talent but not much depth, and everybody knew that San Diego's expansion club, the Padres, would struggle initially. Heck, one of their best players was outfielder Ollie Brown, who couldn't hold down a reserve's job with the Giants.

As the season began, it was obvious that Willie McCovey was on his way to having a fabulous season. He amassed eight home runs and 22 RBIs in April. Then he really started to take off. From May 25 to June 11, he hit .453 (24-for-53) with 11 homers and 21 RBIs. A few teams used a defensive shift on him—kind of like they do for almost every hitter nowadays—featuring three infielders between first and second base and a four-man outfield playing him to pull. Mac always ignored this kind of stuff. His .320 batting average for the season proves that he was still able to get his hits. And, of course, no shift could prevent him from hitting the ball out of the park. Really, the only effective defense to use against Mac was to intentionally walk him. He set a record that year with 45 free passes. McCovey grudgingly appreciated the respect, but he rather would have been allowed to swing the bat. Mac maintained a calm exterior, but one day the following season, he exploded after Cincinnati manager Sparky Anderson ordered him put on base for what seemed like the umpteenth time in a row. On his way to first base, Mac hollered at Sparky, "Who do you think I am, Babe Ruth?"

"No," Sparky yelled back, "you're better."

A couple of other guys had big years. Playing his first full big league season, 23-year-old Bobby Bonds became the youngest player to reach 30 home runs and 30 stolen bases. Juan Marichal won 21 games and led the NL with a 2.10 ERA. All this wasn't quite enough to put the Giants over the top. In the West standings, the Giants, Reds, Braves, and Dodgers took turns occupying first place during September. Even the Astros were mathematically in the race, though they usually were a couple of games behind the top four teams.

A three-game sweep of the Dodgers at Candlestick on the regular season's next-to-last weekend put the Giants in first place with a precarious half-game lead. With that many teams in contention, there was no margin for error. This time it was the Braves' turn to build a long winning streak. They won 10 in a row from September 19–30. Doomed by losses to the last-place Padres on September 23–24, the Giants finished three games behind Atlanta.

1971

This was the last hurrah for the vintage Giants. By the end of 1973, Willie Mays, Willie McCovey, Juan Marichal, and Gaylord Perry all had been traded to cut expenses for owner Horace Stoneham and make the roster more simple for Charlie Fox to manage since he didn't have to deal with the challenge of dealing with any veterans.

The playoff opener against the Pittsburgh Pirates was a classic. Tito Fuentes hit a surprise two-run homer, McCovey hit a more predictable two-run homer, and Perry pitched a gritty complete game in a 5–4 Giants win. But on the next afternoon, Bob Robertson, who relatively few people outside of Pittsburgh had heard of, clobbered three home runs as the Pirates evened the series with a 9–4 win.

Marichal allowed only four hits in Game 3, but two were home runs by Richie Hebner and, of course, Robertson. We couldn't get much offense going and we lost 2–1. Game 4 started out to be wild. We had a 5–5 tie going after two innings, but the Pirates pulled away with four runs in the sixth and won it 9–5.

A lot of people believe that we lost that series in September during the waning weeks of the regular season. We played erratic baseball and were forced to use Marichal on the last day of the season to stay a game ahead of the Los Angeles Dodgers and clinch the division. Had we been able to clinch earlier, we could have opened the playoff with Marichal pitching Game 1 and Perry starting Game 2. Assuming we won both games behind our two aces, getting past Pittsburgh and into the World Series by winning just one of the next three games would have seemed possible, especially since we finished 9–3 against the Pirates during the regular season. That still gnaws at anybody who was associated with the '71 team.

We barely missed out on reaching the World Series in 1971, and it was the last hurrah for the terrific triumvirate of Willie Mays, Juan Marichal, and Willie McCovey.

1987

Humm Baby! What a great year to be a Giants fan. The ballclub ended its 16-year division-title drought behind manager Roger Craig, whose pet phrase, "Humm Baby," became associated with the team as an advertising slogan, rallying cry, statement of praise, or whatever you wanted it to be. The roster was full of Humm Babies, guys who played their butts off—almost literally. I must have set a personal record for sewing and patching the seats of so many uniform pants that guys ripped while sliding into bases or diving for line drives.

The seeds for this club were planted the previous year. Having taken over the club toward the end of the 1985 season, general manager Al Rosen and Craig set about getting rid of the team's many malcontents. Mostly, it was guys who hated playing at Candlestick Park. Rosen and Craig wanted to assemble a team who would be proud to wear the Giants uniform and who would regard Candlestick as a home-field advantage instead of a nuisance.

With first baseman Will Clark and second baseman Robby Thompson, the right side of the infield was prime "Humm Baby" territory. Clark was headed for his first big year of many (.308, 35 home runs, 91 RBIs), and I've seen few players better than Thompson at executing the proverbial little things, such as defense, advancing runners, and stealing bases.

Jeffrey Leonard, Chili Davis, and Candy Maldonado combined their skills to give us a formidable outfield. And our bench with Mike Aldrete, Chris Speier, Bob Melvin, Joel Youngblood, and Harry Spilman was first-rate. But we didn't think we were well-rounded enough. So on July 5, we traded for third baseman

Kevin Mitchell and left-handers Dave Dravecky and Craig Lefferts from the San Diego Padres and gave them third baseman Chris Brown, left-handers Mark Davis and Keith Comstock, and right-hander Mark Grant. Lefferts could fit any bullpen role, Dravecky deepened the starting rotation, and Mitchell gave our offense a little more pop than Brown did. It wasn't as if we gave San Diego a bag of doughnuts; Davis won the Cy Young award two years later.

So we were improved but not complete. That last step occurred on August 21, when we dealt right-handers Scott Medvin and Jeff Robinson to the Pittsburgh Pirates for right-hander Rick Reuschel. That was quite a move by Rosen since the Cincinnati Reds were trying to get Reuschel, too. Now our starting rotation had an ace. Once we put things together, there was no stopping us. We went 37–17 down the stretch to win the division. It seemed like the Giants were destined to win every day.

It seemed like the postseason would go our way, too. We split the first two games of the National League Championship Series at the St. Louis Cardinals. Dravecky pitched an absolutely beautiful two-hit shutout in the second game, but tensions grew higher with each inning. Leonard, the Hac-Man, hacked off the Cardinals with his "one flap down" method of running the bases after hitting home runs. Chili was quoted as saying that St. Louis was a "cow town," which angered Cardinals fans, to say the least. We led the series 3–2 as we went back to St. Louis, but we didn't score a single run in the last two games. St. Louis went to the World Series instead of us. That one really, really hurt mainly because we hadn't reached the postseason in such a long time.

1989

This club was a lot like the '87 team except most of the pieces were in place, and most of the guys who had been with the Giants since '87 were improved. Will Clark batted a career-high .333. Kevin Mitchell, who had become one of the league's premier run producers, hit 47 homers, drove in 125 runs, and was the league's MVP. He moved from third base to left field to accommodate Matt Williams. The Clark-Mitchell-Williams combo at the 3-4-5 spots in the batting order was one of the best in franchise history. Fully entrenched as staff ace, Rick Reuschel made the All-Star team that year. Don Robinson, a trade-deadline acquisition, arrived from the Pittsburgh Pirates. In 1987 he converted to starting and helped solidify the rotation behind Reuschel. When the need arose for a closer, Al Rosen acquired Steve Bedrosian from the Philadelphia Phillies. This time we finished the job in the National League Championship Series, defeating the Chicago Cubs in five games to win the pennant for the first time since 1962.

Just like in that '62 season, nature forced a stoppage in play during the World Series except this one was a lot more serious. The Loma Prieta earthquake struck at 5:04 PM local time just minutes before Game 3 was to begin at Candlestick Park. I was alone in the clubhouse with Robinson, the Giants' Game 3 starter, when the shaking started. After a delay of 10 days to enable the San Francisco Bay Area to regain a semblance of normalcy, the series resumed. Though the Oakland A's, who won the first two games, completed the four-game sweep, I honestly believe that if it hadn't been for the quake, we would have won at least a couple of games in that series. They were too good of a club at home (53–28) not to, and the delay hurt us because it allowed the A's to reset their rotation.

1993

The ache from this season didn't get any easier to bear over the years. This one was tough to swallow because in a way we didn't do anything wrong. We didn't fall short in any way. We finished 103–59, the best record since the franchise moved to San Francisco in 1958. How can anybody call that a failure? We were, however, victims of circumstance. The wild-card playoff format wasn't scheduled to go into effect until 1994 (which didn't happen anyway due to the work stoppage that forced commissioner Bud Selig to cancel the World Series).

I will admit that the Atlanta Braves, who beat us out for the National League West division title by finishing 104–58, played outstanding baseball after they traded for San Diego Padres first baseman Fred McGriff. Atlanta went 53–41 pre-McGriff and 51–17 once he started playing for them. You can't fault our players for not producing enough. Barry Bonds joined us and won the league's MVP award. John Burkett and Bill Swift went 22–7 and 21–8, respectively. Rod Beck converted 48 of 52 save opportunities. Will Clark had what was an off year for him, but he batted .379 in the season's final month. Matt Williams hit 38 homers and drove in 110 runs. Robby Thompson and Kirt Manwaring had their best years. They did all they could, and it hurt to go home after the season ended. It was Dusty Baker's first year as manager, and I thought he did a hell of a job. He seldom got mad at the players, just like Mr. Bochy. And why should Baker have gotten mad? Everybody did all they could.

2000

I didn't include the 1997 team among my long list of "heartbreakers" because they got swept by the Florida Marlins in the National League Division Series. I do think the Giants got the raw end of the deal by winning the division title yet having to begin the series on the road. That glitch in the system, so to speak, later was corrected. By then, of course, it was a little too late for the Giants.

However, the timing seemed right in 2000. It was Pacific Bell Park's inaugural season, and we responded with an excellent season. Our 97–65 record was good enough for another division title. It kind of resembled the 1993 season in that a lot of players stepped up their games. Jeff Kent (.334, 33 home runs, 125 RBIs) established himself as an offensive force. He won the MVP award, the only player to place ahead of Barry Bonds (.306, 49 home runs, 106 RBIs) in the voting. Ellis Burks and J.T. Snow drove in 96 runs apiece. Rich Aurilia announced his presence by hitting 20 home runs. Five starting pitchers—Livan Hernandez, Russ Ortiz, Shawn Estes, Kirk Rueter, and Mark Gardner—won at least 11 games apiece. Robb Nen recorded 41 saves in 46 chances. This ballclub looked poised to advance deep into October.

In came the New York Mets for the National League Division Series. We won Game 1 by a 5–1 score and seemed prepared to grab a huge psychological advantage in Game 2 when Snow tied the score in the ninth inning with a three-run homer off Mets closer Armando Benitez. But the Mets won it 5–4 in the 10th inning before crushing our spirits and our postseason bid when the series moved to New York. We left 16 men on base—*16*—in a 3–2, 13-inning loss in Game 3. We were down, but we weren't out because the Mets' Game 4 starter was Bobby Jones, a soft-tossing right-hander who recorded a 5.06 regular-season ERA. I thought surely we'd chase him with a few early runs. Well, we were lucky just to get a hit. That's right; one measly hit was all we got in a 4–0 loss. Sometimes guys like Jones fool you by dazzling you with those garbage pitches. Frankly, it was sickening to watch.

2002

This was the all-time crusher. I can't deny that. There's no point in analyzing the season. It came down to those last two World Series games in Anaheim, when we went back there leading the Angels three games to two. We were ahead 5–0 entering the seventh inning, feeling pretty good about ourselves. Then Russ Ortiz allowed a couple of one-out singles in the seventh inning. Dusty Baker went to the mound to remove him from the game and gave him the baseball as a souvenir for a job well done. I'm convinced that Baker meant no disrespect toward the Angels with that gesture. I also knew that giving Ortiz the ball was a mistake. We all remember what happened next, as well as what happened the next night. Five outs away from winning our first World Series as San Francisco Giants, we were left at the altar again.

2003

For most fans the enduring memory about the 2003 National League Division Series loss to the Florida Marlins has been the image of J.T. Snow being thrown out at home plate for the final out in Florida's Game 4 clincher, which ended the Giants' ninth-inning rally in their 7–6 loss. Second-guessers like to point out that had the Giants kept speedy outfielder Eric Young on the postseason roster, he could have run for Snow and easily would have scored the tying run.

I have my own indelible memory from this series, and it's not good either. Jose Cruz Jr., who committed two errors all season and won a Gold Glove that year for his defensive excellence, dropped Jeff Conine's catchable fly ball to open the Marlins' 11th inning moments after the Giants scored in the top of the 11th to go ahead 3–2. One thing led to another, and the Marlins scored twice to win it 4–3. They assumed a 2–1 lead in the series, which in a short postseason encounter is so important.

Fortunately, our fate would turn several years down the road.

3

Joining the Club

My world has revolved around baseball for as long as I can remember. I grew up with my parents, three sisters, and one brother near the intersection of 10th and Howard Street in San Francisco's Excelsior District down the street from the old Burgermeister brewery. A lot of kids my age lived there, so there was always a ballgame going on that you could join. I played baseball from sun up to sundown every day.

My father, Richard, was a printer. He used to supply ink to all the newspapers in San Francisco. Plenty of them existed back then. The *San Francisco Chronicle* and *San Francisco Examiner* were rivals then and are still around. When I was eight or nine years old, my dad began taking me to weekend games at Seals Stadium, the ballpark on 16th and Bryant Street, where the Triple A Seals played. Those guys instantly became my heroes. Haywood Sullivan later became general manager of the Boston Red Sox. Something else that made going to the ballpark such an experience were the smells. That's the right, the aroma. The combination was almost too much to describe. Hamm's Brewery, which never seemed to shut down, was adjacent to the ballpark. And the neon beer glass atop the Hamm's building, which magically emptied and refilled itself every few seconds, was a San Francisco landmark. You could see it from almost anywhere in the city. Across the street from Hamm's was a Hostess bakery making bread and cupcakes. Behind the left-field wall, you could smell more sweet stuff coming from Stempel's Quality Doughnut Shoppe. Every day at Seals Stadium smelled like a birthday party.

And the ballpark itself—well, it was so small and intimate that it almost seemed to embrace you. It looked so elegant with its emerald green façade. Russ Hodges, the Giants' Hall of Fame broadcaster, called it a "beautiful little watch charm" in his book *My Giants*. If there was a baseball heaven, that was it.

Getting there was so easy. Just about every bus or streetcar line on the San Francisco Municipal Railway stopped at Seals Stadium or at least had a convenient transfer, which was a good thing because there was no place to park. Ballplayers had to park in a little garage below street level. But not too many guys had cars anyway. They always took the buses or got a cab.

As a kid, I'd stand by the gate in left field during batting practice near Stempel's and next to one of the few parking lots near the ballpark. I'd catch the balls and throw them all back. A fellow named Leo "Doc" Hughes noticed that. Doc was a typical baseball employee of that time. He had not one but three jobs: athletic trainer, traveling secretary, and equipment manager. Anyway, Doc kind of liked me because I threw back all the batting practice homers. One day I happened to be there, and Doc said, "Hey, we need a batboy. Would you like to be a batboy?" I replied, "Heck yes!"

As a batboy with the Seals was how I got started. That was 1955, and I was 13 years old. I loved the yard so much. I got there early every day. There's just something about the ballpark that I loved. I guess that's why I've been in baseball all my life. I wanted to be around ballplayers. They all seemed like decent guys, and, of course, when I was younger, I wanted to be one of them. I played mostly first base and did some catching. I considered myself an average player, but looking back on it, I might have been a little better than I thought. I played for what was known as a Rookie League team composed of older teenagers, some of whom were legitimate prospects. It was no accident that the team was organized by Giants scout Ed Montague, the man who signed Willie Mays.

Sometimes the competition was unbelievable. These were the names of the guys who tried out for this East-West All-Star Game one year: Willie Stargell, Joe Morgan, Jim Fregosi, Pat Corrales, Walt "No-Neck" Williams, Johnny McNamara. Bobby Cox came up from Fresno. It was a four-day event at Big Rec, which is a historic San Francisco ballyard. It was destroyed by fire after the 1906 earthquake and then rebuilt. Anyway, we'd take infield and batting practice and play two games a day amongst each other. One scout I talked to was Charlie Walgren. I met him because he was around Seals Stadium all the time. He said, "Don't worry; I'll call you." But I knew I didn't have a burglar's chance.

Some of those guys became friends. I loved Fregosi for instance. He set every baseball record at Junipero Serra High School in San Mateo, California, was the best player in history at Menlo College a little bit farther down the Peninsula, went on to become a six-time American League All-Star with the California Angels, and then managed the Angels, Chicago White Sox, Philadelphia

Phillies, and Toronto Blue Jays. He later worked for the Giants as an assistant to general manager Brian Sabean after he was done managing. He used to pick on me during those tryouts, but it was all in fun. "Hey, Murph," he'd say, "you're a terrible ballplayer. But at least you try."

Man, oh man, Stargell was terrific. He went from the little town of Alameda in the shadow of Oakland to Cooperstown. He was a first-ballot Hall of Famer, two-time National League home run champion, and the National League MVP. I always loved it when the Pittsburgh Pirates and Giants played and Stargell and Willie McCovey would get together and chat. I'd say, "There's about 900 home runs and 3,000 RBIs sitting over there."

During those East-West tryouts, I watched him hit home run after home run, and it was the same after he reached the majors. He hit 25 homers at Candlestick Park, tying him with Dale Murphy for the most ever by a visiting player. Stargell hit one of the darndest home runs I ever saw at Candlestick. He came to bat one night against Giants right-hander Randy Moffitt, who had been injured and was trying to pitch himself back into shape. Stargell swung and hit this line drive that kept carrying and carrying. It didn't sink, but it didn't climb either. The Cyclone fence in the outfield was eight feet high, and I swear that the altitude of Stargell's hit stayed at about eight or nine feet from the time he made contact until the ball cleared the fence. It was a pure, 410-foot line drive. Unbelievable. Stargell and I got to know each other even better when I was the visiting clubhouse manager at Candlestick, and we always met for lunch when the Giants and Pirates played in either city.

When I was the Seals' batboy, the Pacific Coast League was our world. There were so many talented players in the PCL that it was like a third major league. We didn't give much thought to the real major leagues. I mean, I barely knew who Willie Mays was. But I certainly knew who Ted Williams was—partly because the Seals were a Boston Red Sox affiliate. I remember rushing from school to Seals Stadium to watch Williams play in an exhibition game for the Red Sox against the Seals, but an earthquake canceled the game. It wouldn't be the last time that happened.

When the news came in 1957 that the Seals were no more because the Giants were moving to San Francisco, I cried my eyes out. Jerry Donovan, the Seals' general manager, informed me what was happening. But just as one door closed, another one opened almost simultaneously. "Don't worry," Mr. Donovan said. "We'll get you a job with the Giants. You'll still be a batboy."

Mr. Donovan and Leo Hughes talked to Eddie Logan, who had been the Giants' clubhouse manager since 1947 and was moving West with them. "We've got the right kid for you," they told him. I soon met Mr. Logan, and he seemed to like me a lot. But somebody within the organization also promised a batboy's job to Roy "Red" McKercher. So at first I was the visiting team's batboy. I didn't mind. I would still go to Seals Stadium everyday and still be around the ballplayers! How much more fun could I have?

San Francisco was a big league city before the Giants arrived. Everybody knows that. No city in the United States can match its combination of natural beauty—the hills, the bay—and its man-made attractions such as Coit Tower or the Golden Gate Bridge. But having a major league ballclub like the Giants in your city makes it a little more legitimate. It's like free publicity for the team's home city, which receives extra attention on television and radio broadcasts and through word of mouth. Many San Franciscans liked to believe that they were more sophisticated than the average American and above such ordinary pursuits as baseball. The truth was that baseball had long been almost a natural resource in San Francisco. Just look at the ballplayers who came from the city. The greatest, of course, was Joe DiMaggio. But his brothers Vince and Dom were pretty good big leaguers, too. The list goes on and includes Tony Lazzeri, Bobby Brown, Lefty O'Doul, Joe Cronin, Harry Heilmann, Willie Kamm, Gino Cimoli, Jerry Coleman, Frank Crosetti, and many others. Baseball had established a fairly solid fanbase, too. The Seals set a minor league record in 1948 with a season paid attendance of about 670,000. That record stood for 40 years.

Yet when the Giants came here, it was almost as if the Bay Area rediscovered baseball. The parade that welcomed the team to San Francisco is still regarded as a legendary event. It even made the cover of *LIFE* magazine, which printed a photograph of Mays perched in a convertible greeting a couple of young fans. I, of course, couldn't make it to the parade. I was helping Mr. Logan get the clubhouses ready for the players. Workers were knocking down the left-field wall to add bleacher seats that would increase the seating capacity from 18,500 to about 23,000.

I guess I did a good job that day, and the day after that, and the day after that, and the day after that because Mr. Logan asked me to fill in as the Giants' batboy for midweek day games since McKercher had another commitment on those afternoons. Naturally, I accepted, though I had to jump through hoops to get the job done. I'd be on the visitors' side, performing my batboy duties for the Pirates, Cincinnati Reds, Chicago Cubs, or whoever, and then when the inning ended, I'd dash for the nearest private area and change into a Giants uniform. What's more I had to remember to keep the home-plate umpire stocked with baseballs. People hadn't started using the word "multitasking," but it sure would have applied to me on those days. I did this in 1958–59, the club's first two seasons in San Francisco.

The Giants' first San Francisco ballclub was respectable. Heck, better than that. They finished third in the eight-team National League and even held first place for 32 days before reality—and the Milwaukee Braves—set in. The Giants had excellent lineups mainly because any batting order with Mays somewhere in it is a promising one. But the Braves' pitching outclassed the rest of the league. Warren Spahn, Lew Burdette, and future Giants pitcher Don McMahon were just a few of the pitchers who helped the Braves, the defending World Series champions, win their second pennant in a row.

Still, the Giants didn't have to take a back seat to anyone. Mays batted a career-high .347. First baseman Orlando Cepeda hit .312 with 25 home runs and 96 RBIs and was a unanimous choice for the National League's Rookie of the Year award. Jimmy Davenport established himself as a top-notch third baseman. Johnny Antonelli, Sam Jones, Mike McCormick, and Ruben Gomez, who shut out the Dodgers in the first major league game ever played on the West Coast, formed a decent core for the pitching staff to build around.

And they always—always—played exciting baseball. Consider the game of Monday, May 5, when they got ready to bat in the bottom of the ninth inning while trailing the Pirates 11–1. The Giants loaded the bases with nobody out before Willie Kirkland popped out. Then the fun started. King and Antonelli—yes, the pitcher—hit back-to-back two-run doubles. Bob Speake, the third pinch-hitter in a row used by the Giants, doubled home Antonelli. The Pirates still led 11–6, but Ray Jablonski, whose single led off the inning, belted a three-run homer. Cepeda homered, trimming the Pirates' lead to a single run. The Giants reloaded the bases on two walks, and an error before the game finally ended on Don Taussig's pop-up.

More excitement was in store. I can still remember working late on the night of July 29, 1959, cleaning shoes and handling "wet stuff"—game-used clothing that needed to be laundered. Mr. Logan said that he had to go to the bar across the street, the Double Play, to meet somebody who owed him money. But I know he went over there to have a few "horns" or "belts." Okay, drinks. Bill Rigney, the Giants' manager, was still in the clubhouse. He was always sitting at his desk and was always the last person to leave the clubhouse. He called me over that night and said, "Hey, we're bringing a big Irishman in tomorrow. Wait until you see this guy."

I said to myself, *Wow, an Irish ballplayer for the Giants!* So I got to Seals Stadium extra early the next morning. And when I got to the Giants' clubhouse, my eyes fell out. Sitting alone in front of an empty dressing stall was a ballplayer like none other I had ever seen. He was big all right. I thought Paul Bunyan had come to life. The clubhouse was small to begin with, and this guy took up whatever space was left. But he wasn't Irish unless this guy had escaped from an Irish clan of African Americans that nobody knew about. Staring at the floor, he seemed a little shy at first. But when I went over to shake his hand, he looked straight into my eyes. "Hi, I'm Willie McCovey," he said.

McCovey had spent plenty of time in spring training with the big league club, so while I gathered the gear he needed, including the jersey with the No. 44 that he would make famous, he received greetings from the veterans as they started to arrive for that day's game against the Philadelphia Phillies. "Lovey-dovey McCovey," they yelled, amusing themselves. Pretty soon, McCovey couldn't help but smile. And when he smiled, he lit up the room. I've loved Stretch ever since. "After the game I met Willie Kirkland and Leon Wagner, two of my Giants teammates, for dinner," McCovey said. "There was a newsstand near the restaurant, and the latest edition of the *Call-Bulletin*, an evening newspaper, had details about the game with my name in headlines. That was the first time I had ever seen my name like that, so that was exciting. I think I bought all the papers that were on that stand."

Mac went on to win the Rookie of the Year award, just as Cepeda did in '58. But it was a heartbreaking season. You could say it was the first time I was "left at the altar" like a jilted bride-to-be. The Giants were in first place and had a two-game lead over the Los Angeles Dodgers with eight games left to play. The Dodgers came into town and swept not only a day/night doubleheader, but also the entire three-game series. That seemed to derail the Giants, even though we were still very much alive mathematically. We slumped to third during the season's final week.

I worked at spring training for the first time in 1960. Being 18 years old, I was thrilled. The Giants trained at Second and Mohave near Central Avenue. We stayed at the old Adams Hotel. There were no cars available, so we had to walk to the ballpark. It was a good 15, 20 blocks from the ballpark to the hotel. Nobody rented cars; nobody showed up early. They didn't give cars to ballplayers or anything like they do nowadays. At that time, there were no freeways in Arizona. The first time I went there, there was one road to get down and one road to get back. Either you got off at Baseline Road or the one way down south, Buckeye Road, and you'd go through all the Native American villages.

The following year, the Giants began training in Casa Grande, Arizona. When the Cactus League exhibition season started, they'd return to the Phoenix area. At Casa Grande the Giants built a complex with five baseball diamonds, as well as a resort hotel, a restaurant, and a swimming pool shaped like a baseball bat. Giants owner Horace Stoneham believed it could become a magnet for tourists, but we were still way off the beaten path. It never caught on the way Mr. Stoneham hoped it would. But to be fair, we were decades away from spring training becoming a multi-million dollar industry within an industry.

The ins and outs of spring training weren't easy. There were no washers or dryers in the clubhouse. We used to have to take stuff to downtown Casa Grande and wash it at a laundromat. We had a laundry company come up from Phoenix every day to take the wool uniforms and bring them back the next day. We had another laundry company deliver 1,500 towels every two days. They were small ones. They weren't the big ones you have nowadays. The trainers used them, we used them, the visiting teams used them. We put the ballplayers' duffel bags in front of their lockers, and they'd dig out what they'd need every day. You'd wash the wet stuff and drop it on top of their duffel bag. That's the way it was years ago. There was no food, TVs, or radio in the clubhouse.

Though we'd be at Casa Grande for only a few weeks per year, the Giants' executives did what they could to make the most of their time there. Mr. Stoneham loved talking baseball, often long into the night. That led to the creation of the "Blue Room," which was essentially a lounge where Giants people—from front-office types to Mr. Stoneham's sidekicks to the manager and maybe a coach or two—could gather and quench their thirst. Carl Hubbell, the Hall of Fame left-hander who became the team's minor league director, was a Blue Room regular, explaining why he always requested a room on the extreme end of the first floor. Thus, he'd find it easier to locate his quarters after a long Blue Room session.

Having worked my way up from batboy to clubhouse manager, I work in my office at Pacific Bell Park. (Mike Murphy)

Oh, I used to do everything for everybody, and Mr. Stoneham kept me busy, that's for sure. He would call me in the middle of the night to get him a pack of smokes. This was before there were any 7-Eleven stores around. Where was I going to find cigarettes at 4:00 AM? So I started carrying a couple of extra packs in my suitcase. He said, "Where did you find them?" I said, "Hey, I've got my connections."

Mr. Stoneham called me up one day and asked me if I wanted to make some extra money. He told me that he wanted me to keep an eye on Harvey Kuenn and a couple of other guys to make sure they weren't getting drunk too often because they have to play a ballgame the next day. But I didn't want to squeal on anybody. So when the road trip was over, I gave Mr. Stoneham his money back.

He said, "What's that for?"

I said, "I don't like the job. I'd rather handle just the equipment."

Mr. Stoneham said, "But I need somebody to watch those guys."

"Yeah, but the only trouble is that I went out with those guys and got drunk with them. I don't know what time I came in."

A lot of people might wonder whether moving from Seals Stadium to Candlestick Park for the 1960 season could be considered progress. True, the seating capacity virtually doubled to 42,500, and Mays had a lot more room for chasing fly balls. But that wind—my God. It came hurtling right through Bayview Hill. It seemed like it never stopped. You know how ballplayers somehow keep their hair in place, even though they're wearing caps and they're putting them on and taking them off? It wasn't that way at Candlestick. Everybody's hair got messed up at that place, whether they were ballplayers or spectators.

The odd thing for native San Franciscans was that so many of us had never even heard of Candlestick Point, where the ballpark was built. The only thing I used to see from around there was that big crane in the background that was situated at an old naval shipyard. I had cousins who lived kind of close to the Candlestick construction site on Third Street and Revere Avenue. They used to go fishing there because there was so much marshland. It certainly wasn't the most glamorous location. But Mr. Stoneham wanted a place where 10,000 cars could park. He correctly assumed that a large percentage of fans would drive from the suburbs to see the Giants play. Thus, he needed a ballpark with ample space for parking.

Interestingly, the clubhouses at Candlestick were the first items on the long list of ballpark necessities to be completely constructed. They functioned as the Giants' executive offices until the rest of the park was ready. The park was built on hard rock, which thousands of people would be thankful for about 30 years later when the Loma Prieta earthquake struck minutes before Game 3 of the 1989 World Series was scheduled to begin. After that huge earthquake, there was almost no damage to Candlestick because it sat on hard rock. The only crack was a little piece of concrete up in center field. That's all. As big an earthquake as it was, the park should have tumbled down. But the quake didn't do any damage to the clubhouse except a couple of little cracks.

I had an experience during one spring training that was eye-opening but unpleasant. In the early 1960s, we barnstormed through the south, leaving Arizona to play some exhibition games and maybe make an extra buck in the final week or two before Opening Day. We got to Tennessee and began unloading equipment bags when my boss, Logan, noticed that I had grabbed Mays' equipment bag. Logan said, "Put Willie's bag over here on the side." Then came Orlando's bag. "Put Cepeda's over there, too," Logan said. I saw a pattern. McCovey's bag joined Mays' and Cepeda's gear. So did Juan Marichal's and Jose Pagan's. When I asked Logan what was up, he told me, "They can't stay at the team hotel because it doesn't allow blacks and Latins." Spending all my life in San Francisco, I never heard about that before. The next morning, I went to get coffee and I saw the "Whites Only" signs everywhere. I never wanted to go back to the South.

I didn't just believe in diversity. I lived it. My father was Irish, and my mother was Hispanic. In fact, my real first name is Miguel, though everybody calls me "Mike" and, of course, "Murph." Just that brief, mild exposure to Jim Crow laws was an ugly experience.

My responsibilities seemed to multiply year by year. During the move from Seals Stadium to Candlestick Park before the 1960 season, I continued to help Mr. Logan in the Giants' clubhouse. Shortly before spring training of '61, the visitors' clubhouse manager passed away. I replaced him and kept that job through 1979. I continued to work on the Giants' side during spring training. At first it was tough for me, but with the help of Mr. Logan and everybody, I got over it.

I was earning $100 per month. That might not sound like much to you, but I thought I was the luckiest guy on Earth. Going to the ballpark every day and hanging out with a bunch of great guys? Sometimes I felt like I should have been paying Mr. Stoneham, not the other way around.

Mr. Logan decided to retire before the 1980 season, which is when I became manager of the Giants' clubhouse. I was proud to be so deeply embedded with the franchise I truly loved and the players I deeply respected. I owe an eternal debt to Mr. Logan, who I guess you'd say was my mentor. "The first thing I remember about Murph? My rookie year, 1978. He's the visiting clubhouse guy," pitcher Don Robinson said. "I'm with the Pirates. I'm sitting in the visitors' dugout at Candlestick by the third-base line, and there's all this smoke going up from behind the fence. I say, 'What the hell is going on?' Somebody said, 'Oh, that's Murph. He's cooking us all steaks. Yeah, he puts on sirloins, and that's what we have on getaway day.' Well, that's what Murph does."

The Giants finished over .500 in each of their first 13 seasons in San Francisco. Though we reached the World Series only once in that span, we ranked among the most successful franchises in baseball, if not all of professional sports.

But our fortunes changed dramatically and suddenly. The team's star players grew old almost simultaneously. One year after we won the National League West division title in 1971, we drew 637,327 to Candlestick, which people seemed to dislike more and more because of the wind and the chill. Also—and this doesn't get talked about enough—baseball became kind of irrelevant in San Francisco. A lot of important or just plain scary stuff was happening off the field. The Vietnam War was ending but not very easily. The Zodiac killer and the Zebra murders paralyzed everybody. You had all that weird stuff going on with Patty Hearst's kidnapping and the Symbionese Liberation Army. Joe Amalfitano, one of our coaches, jokingly speculated that the reason the authorities couldn't find Hearst was because she was hiding where nobody ever went—Candlestick's upper deck.

The Giants had a great season in 1978, spending much of the season in first place and drawing 1.7 million to Candlestick. But a sequence of stunning events during a period of less than 10 days in November of that year left Bay Area residents thinking about anything but baseball. Jim Jones, the leader of a religious cult who had numerous ties to San Francisco, ordered the murder/suicide of his followers in Guyana. Then San Francisco mayor George Moscone and Harvey Milk were shot to death at City Hall. Moscone was a huge supporter of the Giants, having backed Bob Lurie's efforts to block the ballclub's sale to investors who would have moved the franchise to Toronto in 1976.

Our fortunes seemed to turn a corner after Al Rosen became general manager and Roger Craig took over as manager following the 1985 season, the only 100-loss year in Giants history. We finished above .500 every year from 1986 to 1990, won two division titles, and reached the World Series in 1989. But in June 1992, voters rejected the Giants' fourth stadium initiative—each of which sought taxpayer funding for a new ballpark.

Investors from the Tampa-St. Petersburg, Florida, area, who had tried for years to secure a major league franchise, swooped in for the kill. A group of investors led by Vince Naimoli reached an agreement in principle to purchase the Giants from Mr. Lurie and move them to Florida. For a while San Francisco appeared to have no hope. Late in the 1992 season, I skipped a road trip to meet with Mr. Naimoli's brother, Raymond, at Candlestick. We went through inventory of everything we had: the baseballs, the bats, the uniforms, even the lockers and who they belonged to. "Those lockers, I know the Giants built them," I said.

"We're going to take them, too," Raymond said.

It was heartbreaking. Mr. Lurie said, "I want you to go to Florida." I said, "No, I don't want to go. I'm a Californian. I was born here and I'll die here. I don't like the heat in Florida anyway. I'm a cold-weather guy. Besides, I'm a third-generation San Franciscan. I love the Bay Area and I always will be here."

As if we needed further dramatics, the television crew that handled Giants telecasts taped a scene, which almost actually happened, in which my dog, Boze, and I leave the Giants' clubhouse for the final time. Turning off the lights and walking through the big double doors, I said to Boze, "I guess we won't see this place anymore." *That* was a genuine tear-jerker that was tough to get through. I sure didn't have to act, I know that.

A huge animal lover, I hold Arby, the clubhouse dog, at Pacific Bell Park in 2001. *(Mike Murphy)*

We all know what followed. Peter Magowan led a San Francisco-based investor group that successfully blocked the Tampa takeover and kept the Giants safe at home. In what was probably the best free-agent signing in sports history, Barry Bonds joined the Giants for the 1993 season and led them to four postseason appearances while pursuing and breaking Hank Aaron's all-time home run record.

What the Giants have done with Oracle Park is remarkable. They revitalized that China Basin/South of Market area so much so that the Golden State Warriors of the NBA decided to situate Chase Center, their new arena, not far away. Magowan had a vision. He wanted a downtown ballpark, he wanted the brick exterior, he wanted people sitting in the upper deck to see across the Bay. Everybody said, "They built it, but they won't draw." But, boy, did we start drawing. We had more than three million in paid attendance in 17 out of 19 seasons. I never dreamed that could happen while I watched the Giants draw crowds of 1,200 during the lean years. I also never dreamed that we would play before 530 consecutive home sellout crowds from October 1, 2010 to July 18, 2017. That's a testament to many factors, including the three World Series titles in a five-year span (2010, 2012, and 2014), our peerless ballpark, and our loyal fanbase.

McCovey deserved to play in front of those packed houses. What a charismatic slugger he was. On top of that, he remained a genuinely nice man until his dying day, which arrived on October 31, 2018. I felt compelled to mention Mac alongside the sellouts because he sat in on most of them, watching from his private box on the broadcasters' level. Stretch witnessed games in silence yet demonstrated his loyalty to the Giants with his presence. I challenge anybody to cite a Hall of Famer who remained as faithful to his ballclub as McCovey was.

Asked about this less than a year before his death, he said, "That's part of being a Giant. I've been a Giant, I like to say, 'all my life really.' I was just a young, naïve teenager when they signed me at 17."

The ballpark at Third and King Streets became a moneymaker for the Giants. And nobody was a better profiteer than Bonds. He immediately electrified the Giants' fanbase and made it possible for the club to approach voters with another ballpark initiative in 1996, which did not request taxpayer funding. The measure passed in a landslide vote, freeing Bonds to do what he did better than anyone else. He might receive just one hittable pitch all game. So he learned to discipline himself to wait until that fat pitch came—and then jump on it.

Long before he put on a major league uniform, of course, Barry seemed destined to perform baseball heroics. His father, Bobby, brought him and his brothers, Ricky and Bobby Jr., to Candlestick. Hints of Barry's talent came through when he'd play with a ball and the glove of his godfather, Mays. The Bonds youths would drive Mr. Logan goofy, but they were okay with me. One of them was bound to become a ballplayer. Their father, a five-tool player if there ever was one, absolutely oozed talent.

Hank Sauer, the Giants' hitting instructor, prayed that the Giants would sign Barry after they drafted him out of Junipero Serra High School in 1982. Obviously, my hopes were high, too. Reportedly, negotiations broke down over the difference of a mere $5,000, prompting Barry to attend Arizona State University. The Pittsburgh Pirates selected Barry sixth overall in the 1985 draft and benefited from the first two of his seven MVP seasons.

It's great to see Barry back here as a Giant. It made me proud to see him rejoin the organization as a special assistant. He should have been here all the time, and I think he belongs in the Hall of Fame.

4

Celebrity Encounters

SOMETIMES I'LL WONDER what's more impressive: working alongside many of the greatest performers ever to step between the foul lines or meeting some of history's most unforgettable people outside of the foul lines. I've had a nice run of both. That second group includes two of history's finest singers, perhaps the top rock 'n' roll band ever, five leaders of the free world, and the Holy Father.

Any individual is lucky just to meet one person like this. Thanks to the Giants, I've often been in the right place at the right time. One year in spring training, we were in Palm Springs, California, to play an exhibition game against the California Angels, and we stayed there overnight because we were going to play the San Diego Padres in Yuma, Arizona, the next day. Eddie Logan couldn't make those long bus rides anymore, so I was on the trip. Willie Mays approached me and said, "I'm going out to dinner tonight. You want to join me?"

I said, "Okay, where are we going?"

He said, "Don't worry about it. Call me when you're ready."

A clubhouse attendant often has so much work to do after a day game that he works right up until the usual dinner hour. So I had to rush to get ready to see Mays. I was clean but not 100 percent groomed when I called Mays and told him, "I'm back at the hotel."

Mays said, "Great, I'll pick you up right away."

I said, "How do you want me to dress?"

He said, "Oh, just wear a sport coat."

So we got in the car, drove past all the restaurants, country clubs, and golf courses, and got on Frank Sinatra Way. I said, "Where are we going?" Mays said, "We're going to somebody's house for dinner."

Then he paused before adding, "I think you'll like him."

Finally, we parked near this house, and I asked, "Who owns this place?"

Mays said, "Frank Sinatra."

I said, "You've got to be kidding me."

Suddenly, I started worrying about whether I'd measure up. I told Mays, "I didn't shave or nothing."

Mays said, "You look all right, Skinner. [They called me "Skinner" because I was as thin as a rail.] You look all right."

Sinatra greeted us at the door. He couldn't have been nicer. He made you feel comfortable—like you were one of his guys. He treated me like gold (the same color as all those records on the walls). He showed me around and introduced me to the other guests. Among them was Chicago Cubs manager Leo Durocher. I knew "Mr. Leo" well because of our mutual friendship with Mays and his trips to Candlestick Park. Also present was restaurateur Jilly Rizzo, Sinatra's longtime friend. I was living in a dream world, getting to meet Sinatra. Later on, I heard that Sinatra quizzed Mays briefly about me. "Who is he?" The Chairman of the Board asked.

"That's one of your guys," Mays said. "Skinner plays all your music."

Sinatra said, "Well, I'm glad somebody listens to it because I don't."

Meanwhile, I didn't know what fork to use. But it wasn't a real fancy dinner. Before we started eating, Sinatra held the breadbasket and announced, "In my family it's a tradition that a first-time guest breaks the bread first." So he passed me the basket, I took a piece, and everybody started going pretty good. We mostly talked baseball that night. Once you get Mays started on baseball, you can't stop him.

I had other encounters with Sinatra. Years later, Mays told me that Sinatra was having a party for his birthday. I made him a couple of jerseys and a Giants jacket with his name on it. Not long after that, I saw Los Angeles Dodgers manager Tommy Lasorda on the field. "Hey, Murph, get over here!" Lasorda told me. "How dare you send Frank a Giants uniform!"

I said, "I did it just as a favor. That's all."

Lasorda said, "He's not a Giants fan! He's a Dodgers fan! He bleeds Dodger blue."

So I let Lasorda keep ranting and raving and finally said to him, "Frank told me his favorite color was orange."

Lasorda didn't know what to say. But it's true that orange really was Sinatra's favorite color, and Sinatra actually rooted for the Giants when they played in New York. So when we asked him to throw the ceremonial first pitch before the 1977 home opener at Candlestick Park, we made another specially monogrammed Giants jacket for him. On the left breast of the jacket, it read: "Francis Albert Sinatra/Honorary Coach." That got under Lasorda's skin, too.

I often put Sinatra on the clubhouse stereo when I was working. "Some of my favorite Murph stories always seem to involve Frank Sinatra," said former Giants reliever Javier Lopez. "He knew him along with other crooners like Tony Bennett. We would go into his office, and he'd show me all the photos that he'd taken over the years of service to the Giants. When you walked in there, it was a shrine to sports and entertainment. He has given me various pieces of memorabilia, but my favorite might be a sport coat that Frank Sinatra wore when he hosted a golf tourney. Murph gave it to me because he knew I'd appreciate it. And I do."

I've played Sinatra less in the last few years so the players can hear what they want, which is mostly all that rap music that I don't care for. On Sunday mornings Buster Posey still asks me, "Hey, Murph, where's the Sinatra music?"

There's a Tony Bennett suite down the right-field line at Oracle Park where the Giants play. As you might expect, it's decorated with Bennett-related memorabilia, such as vintage album covers. If it was up to me, the entire suite level would be named for him. Bennett has sung his signature hit, "I Left My Heart in San Francisco," several times at Giants games. For us natives of The City, it's like our national anthem. I never get tired of hearing that song, and he never gets tired of singing it. I think his most meaningful rendition of the song occurred at the Giants' 1993 home opener, which was the first one during Peter Magowan's tenure as managing general partner after he led a successful bid to prevent the Giants from moving to Tampa/St. Petersburg, Florida. This was a euphoric day for a lot of Giants fans, and Bennett delivered the song in perfect Bennett fashion, smiling all the way from the first note to the last.

I had the pleasure of meeting Bennett years ago through the Swig family, who owned the Fairmont Hotel. That's where he first sang "I Left My Heart in San Francisco" in 1961, and it made his career. I didn't see that show, but I saw him in later performances. Like Frank Sinatra, he never disappoints.

When Bennett's at the ballpark, he comes in the clubhouse and says hello to everybody. The last time was for a celebration of his 90th birthday in 2016. And he always stops by my office. He called me for an autographed baseball from Posey a couple of years back, and I sent it to him. Our rapport deepened when I saw him playing tennis at the Hilton hotel in Pittsburgh after the Swigs had introduced us. We sat in the lobby and talked for about an hour. We just talked about baseball. He's a huge baseball buff. "I'd go back to the clubhouse during a game to get something," former infielder Mark DeRosa said, "and I'd see Tony Bennett sitting in Murph's office or Steffi Graf and Andre Agassi or Joe Montana."

That's one of the things I took pride in. You never knew who might show up in my office. Quarterback Alex Smith dropped by for a promotional visit a day or two after he signed his $49.5 million contract with the San Francisco 49ers as the first overall pick in the 2005 NFL Draft. It just so happened that I was several feet away outside of the office, trying to fix or assemble something. So I didn't completely hear what was being said, but every several seconds, somebody—usually Mays—would make a remark that prompted peals of laughter. Smith probably was being teased about his slender build, his princely salary, or his youthful looks. (Mays told Ken Griffey Jr. after the latter had accumulated 10 years in the major leagues that he had underwear older than Griffey was.) I've got to say this for Smith: he took the ribbing really well. He just stood there and grinned.

I didn't meet The Beatles when they visited Candlestick Park for their final concert on August 29, 1966, though I did catch glimpses of them. My job was to show them the layout of the visitors' clubhouse, where they stayed until the concert started. They came straight to Candlestick Park from the airport after performing in Los Angeles the night before. They didn't talk much. Their agent, who was an Englishman, did all the talking. Anyway, this gentleman told me, "We don't want anybody in the clubhouse."

We still fixed the clubhouse up nice for them. We put beds and a curtain in there in case they needed a nap, but I doubt they got any rest. Even though I stood in front and wasn't supposed to let anybody in, they had plenty of visitors. Joan Baez was there with her sister, Mimi Farina. So were Jerry Garcia and Mama Cass. Ralph Gleason, the famed music critic for the *San Francisco Chronicle* who cofounded *Rolling Stone* magazine a year later, also kept the band company.

What's kind of funny is that the itinerary for The Beatles' final tour sounded like one of the road trips taken by the absent

Giants, who again were competing for the National League pennant. Among The Beatles' stops were Cincinnati's Crosley Field, St. Louis' Busch Stadium, New York's Shea Stadium, and Los Angeles' Dodger Stadium. The plan was for The Beatles to leave Candlestick in a two-ton armored truck that would take them through the center-field gate from second base, where the elevated stage was situated. Matty Schwab, the Giants' groundskeeper, wasn't having any of that. The car's tires would have put huge divots in the outfield grass that would have been impossible to fix before the ballclub returned home on September 9. They decided to lay down some plywood that the truck could drive on toward the warning track, which would lead to The Beatles' exit.

In many ways, it was not a typical concert. The Beatles neither rehearsed nor went through the paces of a sound check. Though I didn't see the concert, I read that these were the songs the band performed: "Rock 'n' Roll Music," "She's A Woman," "If I Needed Someone," "Day Tripper," "Baby's in Black," "I Feel Fine," "Yesterday," "I Wanna Be Your Man," "Nowhere Man," "Paperback Writer," and "Long Tall Sally." They performed those 11 songs in 30 minutes. They did the show and they were gone. Attendance was around 25,000, and tickets were only $4.50. The public didn't know what The Beatles already knew: that they planned to stop touring after this excursion. Otherwise, the audience would have been much, much more raucous.

During spring training in Casa Grande, Arizona, in 1976, I was sitting outside the clubhouse, making rosin bags out of old sanitary socks. It was about 3:00 PM, and workouts were over. Everybody was playing golf. Some guy pulled up in an old jalopy. Holy Christ, it was making banging noises. The driver got out and had a light beard, which was probably about a week's worth of growth. He wore a hat and grubby clothes. I said to myself, *I know this guy from somewhere.* And the voice seemed recognizable, too. He asked, "Are the guys training today?"

When I told him they had finished training, he asked me if the bar was open. "Okay," he said. "I'm gonna go to the bar and have a beer."

I asked one of the men who worked at the training complex who that guy was. He said, "That's John Wayne. He comes here all the time. His ranch is just a few miles away."

I should've known. I'm a big John Wayne fan. He sat at the bar with Rocky Bridges, our Triple A manager, who introduced us. Bridges got to know John Wayne when he played and coached for the California Angels. Bridges was a big beer drinker. So was I back then. Shortly afterward, I decided that it was time for a cocktail, but that wasn't the first order of business. I felt that I owed a very big man a very big apology. I approached the larger-than-life figure and said, "I'm sorry, Mr. Wayne. I didn't recognize you."

He said, "That's all right. Just call me John."

Later that spring, John hosted a barbecue for the Giants. I happened to be standing near him when right-hander John D'Acquisto, our hardest-throwing pitcher, approached. Noticing Wayne, D'Acquisto began swaggering over to the actor. It was a perfect imitation of the way Wayne walked. D'Acquisto sounded like Wayne, too. Sticking out his hand to offer a handshake,

D'Acquisto said, "Well hello, pilgrim. It's nice to meet ya." The real John Wayne got a big laugh out of this.

I've met five presidents, beginning with President Reagan. We met for the first time when he was governor of California. He attended maybe one game at Candlestick Park each homestand. Horace Stoneham's secretary would say, "Governor Reagan is coming on Saturday. Could you escort him down the tunnel? Be there at 10:30 AM." I did that all the time for him.

President Reagan had an excellent memory. We were staying at the Bellevue-Stratford Hotel in Philadelphia when I heard that the president was appearing there for something. I phoned Hank Greenwald, the broadcaster who I used to call "Griswold," and told him that the president was coming. "I'll betcha he'll want to see me," I said.

"Nah, he won't stop," Greenwald said.

So we went to the lobby and joined one of the crowds of people that had formed. Eventually, the president, surrounded by Secret Service agents, arrived. It looked like he was going to whisk past us. I hollered, "Hi, Mr. President!"

He said, "Murph! How are you doing? How are the Giants doing?"

"Oh, fine," I replied.

"Great, Murph! Keep up the good work!"

Greenwald couldn't believe it.

Bob Bolin, one of our top right-handers in the 1960s, attended a conference in Charlotte, North Carolina, where President Reagan was speaking. Bolin had the opportunity to meet the president backstage. Somehow it came up in conversation that Bolin had pitched for the Giants, and the president immediately said, "The Giants! Murph! I know Murph!"

Reagan told Bolin about becoming steadily refrigerated at a chilly Candlestick Park game, which forced him to seek self-preservation. Just as Reagan was about to leave, an usher arrived with a comfortable parka that I had sent. "That saved my life," Reagan said.

I met George H.W. Bush after he was out of office through Dennis Liborio, the Houston Astros' clubhouse manager. Liborio told me one day when the Giants were in Houston, "I want you to meet somebody. Come over at about 6:30."

There was President Bush. I shook his hand and everything. He asked me what I did. I told him, "I'm an equipment manager like Dennis Liborio."

He said, "Oh, that's great! How are you doing? Everything else okay?" We posed for a picture, and he put his arms around me and Liborio and said, "If I ever own a ballclub, I want you two guys to come work for me."

Then, on an off-day in Houston, Liborio said the president wanted us to come to his house for lunch. He had a baseball quiz prepared for us. If we answered it right, we got a photograph of an American flag made of red, white, and blue baseballs, which he signed for us. Of course, we answered the questions correctly.

I met the younger George Bush when he was in office. George W. Bush was having a reception for Willie Mays sometime during his first term as president. I had to send him some autographed baseballs. He wrote me a nice letter inviting me to the White House. So I went to the White House. The secretary took care of me, and I got to meet him.

I met President Clinton twice. The first time was at a reception in San Francisco. He came to play golf with Mays at the Olympic Club for Mays' birthday. Then I was Mays' guest at the reception. The next time he came by Shea Stadium to see Barry Bonds. All the players were standing by their lockers, and he shook everybody's hand.

Of course, I met President Obama when the Giants visited the White House the year after the Giants won the 2010 World Series. Our bus pulled up to the White House, and someone was standing on the front steps when the bus pulled up. It was Willie Brown, the former mayor who got our ballpark built.

Thanks to Bill Neukom, who's at the top of his profession as Microsoft's top lawyer, we had the honor of visiting the Supreme Court after that same 2010 World Series win. He knew Justice Anthony Kennedy, which was how we earned that privilege. Court wasn't in session, but all the justices were there, hosting a reception for the entire team. We got to sit in the gallery and in that big, long chamber of theirs. Justice Kennedy spoke, welcoming us all. We walked into the chamber, and the justices gave us a big hand. One of the justices, Sonia Sotomayor, couldn't stop talking about Orlando Cepeda. They're both Puerto Rican.

One of the biggest days in Candlestick Park's entire history was September 18, 1987, when Pope John Paul held Mass before an overflow crowd. Attendance was estimated at 70,000. I didn't know you could fit that many people in there. We used the home clubhouse for the Holy Father. It was an off day for the Giants, enabling utility infielder Chris Speier to receive communion. Though the Pope was in the clubhouse for only a few minutes, I wasn't sure how to behave around him. It wasn't as if he was going to ask me for directions to the batting cage. But I learned fast. In a situation where I might usually shake his hand, I kissed his ring. You had to. You don't shake hands. That was proper protocol. Maybe I'm blessed to go to heaven now.

The Pope quickly went about his business. His entourage slipped his robes and vestments over him. They carried all his stuff, helped him into the bulletproof Popemobile at the right-field bullpen, and drove him to the pulpit near second base.

I met a great friend, the generous restauranteur Don Carson, when he was in Scottsdale, Arizona, with the Charros, a booster group. He also parked cars at some nightclubs I used to go to. When I saw a sign for Don & Charlie's, I went in there and had dinner. I guess you can say that I demonstrated the same faith in Don & Charlie's that I did for the Giants because I ate dinner there every night I spent in Scottsdale during spring training. I went to not only the same restaurant, but also the same table (303). "He's the Cal Ripken Jr. of Don & Charlie's," Carson said.

I savored the lively spring training scene at Don & Charlie's, where on any given night you might see then-commissioner Bud

Selig, Los Angeles Dodgers legend Tommy Lasorda, the ever-popular Dusty Baker, and all-around baseball celebrity Bob Uecker sitting within feet of another yet at separate tables.

Even without the walls and ceiling, which were festooned with sports memorabilia, it was the closest resemblance to Toots Shor's, the iconic Manhattan saloon and eatery that sports figures frequented in the 1950s and 1960s. Much to the delight of the Giants' beat reporters, Carson catered lunches in the Scottsdale Stadium media lounge for many years. But that all ended in 2019, Don & Charlie's final year in its Camelback Road location. Carson agreed to sell the land to a group that is building a hotel on the site. Nothing, of course, ever will come between me and my friendship with Carson.

Robin Williams used to attend games somewhat regularly, especially during the postseason. Maybe that's why we played well in those big games. He'd have everybody in stitches, which must have loosened up our players. One year Williams brought his friend and fellow comedian, Billy Crystal, with him to a postseason game. Williams seemed a little concerned about entering the Giants' clubhouse. But Joe Torre, who worked for the commissioner's office and served as their pregame escort, put Williams' fears to rest. "I know Murph," Torre said.

Williams also showed up at spring training one day with one of his sons. I set it up so his son could be a batboy for a day. Williams said, "What am I going to do?"

I said, "Well, there's an old saying: you have to stay and help." So he gathered shoes, picked up towels, hung up laundered uniforms,

My friend and Giants fan, Robin Williams, visits the Giants' clubhouse in 1991. (Mike Murphy)

etc. By the end of the afternoon, he said he was worn out from working all day. But he had everybody laughing. I enjoyed a nice rapport with Williams. On one of those days when he and Crystal showed up, Williams said, "Murph's the greatest clubhouse manager there ever was."

A huge New York Yankees fan, Crystal cited my Yankees counterpart: "Nah, Pete Sheehy was."

Speaking of Yankees greats, Joe DiMaggio is among the top individuals I met outside of baseball. By the time we crossed paths, he had finished playing and had crossed over—at least in the public's eye—into being well-known as a Mr. Coffee spokesman and Marilyn Monroe's husband. I drove DiMaggio around during a few offseasons in the late 1960s and early 1970s. Our mutual connection was Lefty O'Doul, a legendary figure in San

Francisco baseball who starred with and managed the Seals. Lefty played 11 years in the majors, won two batting titles, and hit .349. That's the highest career batting average for any Hall of Fame-eligible player who's not enshrined. He also was influential in the development of baseball in Japan. Many experts believe that Lefty belongs in Cooperstown for his variety of achievements. I wholeheartedly agree.

DiMaggio's primary destination was Bay Meadows racetrack in San Mateo, California, when he was in town. He sat in the press box for privacy's sake. I knew when to keep my mouth shut, which was basically all the time. As was the case with the Seals, when I never asked for anything and was rewarded with the batboy's job, my restraint impressed DiMaggio. He asked me one day, "Murph, do you have an autographed ball from me?"

I did not. So he signed a ball with an inscription: "Eddie was a good clubhouse guy; you're a GREAT clubhouse guy."

Comedians like the aforementioned Robin Williams and Billy Crystal blend easily into baseball's fabric. Humor is a basic part of the game. Ballplayers need a laugh to relieve tension and break up the monotony of the long season, and Gaylord Perry was a beauty. We'd pretend to get in fights and arguments just to keep everybody on their toes. Perry would say, "Hey, Murph, I can't find my shorts."

I'd reply, "You dummy, they're hanging in your locker."

"No, they're not. You're a lousy clubhouse attendant." And so on.

For a while, I was an unwitting pawn in a scheme that lined the pockets of "The Greaser," as I called him. On road trips I was responsible for unloading the players' equipment bags, and on more than one occasion, Perry would give me $20 to make sure his bag hit the luggage carousel first. "I've got an important appointment," he said.

I had no idea that Perry was organizing pools among the players, which would pay off the individual whose bag emerged first. By getting to me, The Greaser was earning about $400 or more per shot. I eventually got fined by the other players in Kangaroo Court and had to return the money that Perry gave me. Nevertheless, I loved The Greaser.

Hal Lanier was known as a "red ass," somebody who would get mad easily, especially after making some sort of mistake. After a rough game, in which he committed a couple of errors and went hitless at the plate, he vented his frustration by shattering his batting helmet. The batboy came up with all the pieces, so I put them in a box. When December rolled around, I called his wife and told her I had a package for her husband for Christmas. I sent it to her. She said, "My, it's broken."

I said, 'Yeah, your husband did that."

I put a little note on it that said: "Remember me?" He opened it, cursed a little bit, and threw it in the garbage. But I had told his wife to save it for me. So before spring training the next year, when pitchers and catchers reported first, I told his roommate, a right-hander named Ron Herbel, about the whole thing. One night just as Lanier reported to camp, Herbel let me in, and I fixed the helmet up nice and put it underneath his pillow. Herbel told me Lanier got in at about 11:00 PM and was getting ready for bed when he saw the helmet. Apparently, Lanier was enraged, F-bombing everybody. He went in some direction from Casa Grande, Arizona. There weren't too many places to go from there, and apparently he hid it somewhere in the desert. I tried to find it, but Lanier had finally put the helmet to rest.

We played gags on everybody—not just Lanier. On getaway days, whether we were leaving or coming home or going to a different town, left-hander Kirk Rueter stood in the rear of the clubhouse, combing his hair. We'd say, "Why are you in here combing your hair? You ain't got much. You ain't got nuthin'."

Nicknamed "Woody," Rueter used to get mad about it because, well, his hair really was thinning. So I picked up on that and clipped articles from magazines and newspapers about baldness, hairdos, and comb-overs. Then I gave them to a friend, who's a traveling salesman, and he'd send these envelopes to Woody from all over the country. Rueter got mad and told me, "I want to catch this guy who's sending all this stuff."

The Kangaroo Court is a thing of the past now, but it was always a source of amusement. Guys seem to get sensitive very easily these days, which wouldn't make them very good plaintiffs in Kangaroo Court. What happened was that every few weeks, players were fined for mostly minor but embarrassing indiscretions, such as being seen with a woman who was considered unattractive (yeah, it was kind of sexist) or bringing your wife with you to the hotel bar on the road (a longtime universal no-no).

If adjudication is necessary, a full session of the Kangaroo Court was held typically before or after batting practice or during a rain delay. The judge, who often wore a wig fashioned out of the business end of a mop, presided over the meeting. Usually, the judge was a star player who nobody would think about contradicting. For example, in days gone by, Willie McCovey was the Giants' judge. Later on, it was Rich Aurilia. Right now, the Kangaroo Court does not exist in the Giants' clubhouse.

Another long-lasting tradition that has been done away with by law enforcement was a staple of trips to Chicago, which remains a popular spot among baseball people in both leagues. A rite of passage for rookies was to clamber up the statue of general Philip Sheridan near Lakeshore Drive and paint over the...uh...private parts of Sheridan's anatomically correct horse in team colors. I contributed to the hilarity. The morning after the Giants' rookies fulfilled their obligation, a couple of Chicago police officers would show up in the visitors' clubhouse at Wrigley Field to "arrest" the players. I was the one responsible for sending in the officers, who had no intention of actually performing an arrest. In recent years, however, the city of Chicago has cracked down on anybody defacing the statue, which has killed the tradition.

Two of the most amusing Giants I knew were Bobby Bonds and Jim Davenport, who lived in the suburb of San Carlos, California, and did almost everything together. They were like twins. They didn't intend to perform a comedy routine after they retired from playing and became Giants instructors. They just behaved that way. They'd arrive at the clubhouse in San Francisco considerably later than Davenport would have preferred. He'd be fuming. "Hell," Davenport would say, though his thick Southern accent made it sound like "hail." "Hail, Murph, oh, hail, I had to drive Miss Daisy around all day," Davenport said. "We had to go get cigarettes. We had to go make a bet on a horse. Then we had to stop at the club and book our golf game for tomorrow."

Sometimes the joke was on the Giants. Horace Stoneham always thought he could take St. Louis Cardinals legend Stan Musial out to dinner when the Cardinals were in town, get him drunk, and render him unable to play the next day. This trick might have worked once, but it didn't work too often. Musial's career batting average in San Francisco was .306 in 49 games.

It could be argued that Musial is among the most underrated superstars in sports history. Nobody outside of St. Louis talks about him much anymore. Yet he won seven batting titles, hit .331, and finished with 475 home runs, combining power with consistency as few others did.

Willie Mays scoffed at the notion that anybody would regard Musial lightly. "He wasn't underrated to us," Mays said. "He could hit, man. I never saw him hit the ground. A guy would throw at his head; he'd just bend over and keep hitting."

5

2010

We were just a day or two from breaking camp in spring training of 2010. We spent 43 days in Arizona, and that's not counting my getting there a week or so before camp officially opened. I couldn't believe the time went by that fast. You know why it seemed that way? It was the players, the nucleus of guys that we had. We finished 88–74 in 2009 after four losing seasons in a row, so we were on the rise. Tim Lincecum, Matt Cain, and Jonathan Sanchez were starting pitchers with great stuff. Brian Wilson was already a top closer. What a smart guy he was, too. He could do *The New York Times* crossword puzzle in 10 minutes. Maybe we didn't have the best lineup, but guys were always ready to play. Juan Uribe kept everybody going. He jumped on people but in a good way. He'd say, "Come on, let's win."

On this particular spring training day, Jim Davenport and Joey Amalfitano came to visit me. They were primarily minor league instructors, but they dropped by every so often. I went way back with those guys. Davvy was an original Giants player, who was a rookie third baseman in 1958, the team's first year in San Francisco. Amalfitano—I called him "Louie"—was a Giants bonus baby in 1954 who played infield and was on the coaching staff for a couple of years. We started talking about the ballclub, and the more I talked, the more excited I got. "This is the most close-knit Giants team I ever saw," I said.

I saw them glance at each other. I knew they were skeptical. Keep in mind: Davvy and Amalfitano had spent about 100 years in baseball between them. They were smart enough to know that "the best" or "the worst" or "the most" rarely comes around in the game. Heck, they were teammates with Willie Mays. That's all the baseball education you need! Besides, they knew that I had seen every Giants club since the franchise moved to San Francisco in 1958. I had to be overlooking a ballclub or two, right? Even after I said, "This club's gonna go all the way. I can feel it," they kept their mouths shut. "Who would know better than Murph?" Amalfitano told a club insider. "He has the pulse of that clubhouse. He sees what goes on that the trainers don't see—even the managers or coaches don't see. He has his eyes and ears open all the time. In that job you have to."

I often spoke to Tim Flannery, the Giants' third-base coach from 2007 to 2014. "For Murph to make that call shows that he knew the dynamics of what we needed," Flannery said. "That's one of the reasons he has a clubhouse named after him. He's definitely in touch with it all."

I saw what general manager Brian Sabean was trying to do. He believed that effective pitching could lift the Giants to greater heights. Selecting Cain in the first round back in 2002 was the first step. Two more inspired first-round picks followed: Lincecum in 2006 and Madison Bumgarner in 2007. Although many teams regarded Lincecum as a hard-throwing anomaly who risked blowing out his arm with his high-effort delivery, others such as the Giants recognized the good sense behind all those moving parts in his pitching motion. Bumgarner threw slightly across his body, and the Giants could hardly care less. They correctly sensed that the 6'4", 215-pounder had the potential to develop into a monstrous left-hander who could win with power, will, and intimidation.

Sabean envisioned that this rotation would be backed by a bullpen—not necessarily of *hard* throwers but of *strike* throwers, who would use the bayside ballpark's spacious dimensions and the ballclub's excellent defense to its advantage. Hence the Giants signed Jeremy Affeldt in the 2008–09 offseason and drafted the likes of Wilson in the 24th round in 2003 and Sergio Romo in the 28th round in 2005. In succeeding years the Giants added Javier Lopez, Santiago Casilla, George Kontos, Yusmeiro Petit, Guillermo Mota, Ramon Ramirez, and others who rarely beat themselves by throwing ball four.

During a long chat with me in Scottsdale, Arizona, during the spring after the first world title, Affeldt confirmed my happy suspicions. "All of a sudden, you went from a team that didn't have an identity in '08, to finding that identity in '09, to going and getting guys in 2010 that understood what it meant to be a big leaguer and succeed at a big league level," Affeldt said, "and do it with energy and do it with an attitude of: we're not intimidated by anybody, we're not intimidated by any pitchers, we're not intimidated by any hitters because we had guys like Cain and Lincecum in their prime who were not afraid of anybody. And then you had our bullpen, and we weren't afraid of anybody. And then you had these position players come in; a couple of them had won World Series before or had been in the playoff hunt. And now you've found that winning identity. We've got humor, we've got seriousness, we've got knowing when to joke around off the field to do your job on the field, not to take every loss as, 'Oh my gosh, I'm going to get sent down.'"

Affeldt really understood where I was coming from. "Think about it: in 2002 they should have won the World Series," he told a club insider. "And think about how many guys that Murph saw come through there, how many good big leaguers: Willie Mays, Willie McCovey, Will Clark, Dave Dravecky. For Murph to see all those personalities and say, 'I think this team has it,' that's just straight street cred right there. A guy that's seen this clubhouse day-in and day-out for 50, 60 years, he's seen so many potentially good teams that for him to say, 'This is something different,' he feels the environment, he feels the energy. He feels how guys are behaving when they come into the clubhouse. He sees how these guys are coming and going day-in and day-out and he can see whether they're not caring or are caring. What are their personalities? What do they strive to be like? How do they treat us as clubhouse guys? If anybody's going to have any kind of sure knowledge on what he feels can actually happen, it would be a guy like Murph because that guy hasn't seen history from the outside in or just watched it on TV or watched all these players at the ballpark. He has *lived* with these players 10 hours a day, including some of the best players ever to play the game. So for him to have felt that, that doesn't surprise me because I totally believe that he did feel that. He's not a guy who's going to say something because it's the right thing to say. He wouldn't say something like that unless he truly believed it."

What I sensed from these guys besides impressive talent was what Mr. Neukom liked to refer to as "Giants DNA"—players' dedication to their craft, an obligation to the fans, and, most of all, a passion for winning.

The ballclub won six of its first seven games, and everything seemed great. For most of the first three months of the season, we were just off the pace—like a good racehorse—in the National League West. We were pitching about as well as expected. Aubrey Huff, our new first baseman, was off to a good start. Second baseman Freddy Sanchez provided a spark after returning from an injury in mid-May. And Uribe drove in some big runs. I told manager Bruce Bochy, "You've got a good ballclub here now." He replied, "I know I do."

But we needed a little something extra to fend off the Los Angeles Dodgers, who were always competitive, and the San Diego Padres, who were in first place and didn't seem like they would fade. The Colorado Rockies also looked tough. So in May we signed left fielder Pat Burrell, who had been released by the Tampa Bay Rays after being miscast as a designated hitter. He really helped us get over the hump. He played all those years in Philadelphia, where the Phillies knew how to scrap. Outfielder Nate Schierholtz told me, "The whole team's attitude kind of changed when he got here. It seemed like things took off." I read a comment by Dave Hollins, one of Burrell's Philadelphia teammates that summed it all up: "Don't let the pretty face fool you. He's tougher than that face will tell you."

Travis Ishikawa, a Giants first baseman during three different stints with us in 2006, 2008–10, and 2014–15, concurred. "You come back from a tough loss the night before, [and] guys like

Pat and Uribe make sure that we're focused on the game at hand. We're not allowing that tough loss to affect us," he said. "Those are the kind of guys who keep the team solidified, I believe. We could've been on a five, 10-game losing streak, and Uribe would be singing—I want to say it was Latin Christian music and even "O Canada"—and keeping everything light. You don't have time to feel down or have a pity party because things aren't going your way. Everything's so light and lively that we're loose and ready to go for the next game."

Burrell was a key addition, which helped bolster our strong team chemistry. "There was such a brutal honesty to that clubhouse that was so refreshing," said Mark DeRosa, a Giants utilityman in 2010–11. "Bruce Bochy would always say, 'Hey, I'm going to have an open-door policy. You guys can come in any time you want. You might not always like what you're going to hear.' I felt like our clubhouse was an extension of that. If you come into the clubhouse, you're going to know exactly how everyone feels about you—one through 25. There were pockets of great characters on that team like Pat Burrell. If Pablo got out of line, Renteria would reel him back in. If Rowand got out of line, Burrell would set him straight."

It was a combination of young and old players that melded perfectly. "Looking at the club, I think it was the perfect blend of veterans and younger talent," Lopez said. "The stars were young and respectful of the vets in the room. We all had a great relationship, and when things went bad, the younger players got their cue from the veterans. A lot of them had been stars on other teams and or won a World Series and knew what it would take. I think the biggest thing was that everyone bought in. It was never questioned. All we wanted to do was win that day, and if we didn't, forget it quickly and move on."

All that was great, but still we needed more. So on July 1, we traded Bengie Molina to the Texas Rangers. This enabled Buster Posey, who as a rookie was already showing signs of greatness, to become the starting catcher. He had been filling in at first base and behind the plate. Granted, everybody—and I mean everybody from the front-office executives to the players to the stadium maintenance workers—understood what an asset Molina was, given his hitting ability and knowledge of the pitching staff. More than that, Molina was a lovable guy. However, Posey was an irresistible force. Promoted to the Giants from Triple A one month before the Molina trade occurred, Posey got three hits in each of his first two games while driving in four runs. "Here comes Jesus Christ," Huff hollered after one of those games when Posey entered the clubhouse. I don't think Posey appreciated that kind of humor. But he got used to it quickly enough.

In danger of falling out of the National League West race, we trailed San Diego by seven-and-a-half games after losing in 15 innings at Colorado on July 4. But then we caught fire. Our record for the rest of July was 19–5, a stretch which began with us sweeping the Milwaukee Brewers in a four-game series on the road. Home or away, three guys carried us through the entire month: Huff, Posey, and Andres Torres. Each compiled an OPS (on-base percentage plus slugging percentage) that exceeded 1.000, which was remarkable. They produced runs with equal efficiency: Huff had eight homers and 23 RBIs, Posey accumulated seven homers and 24 RBIs, and Torres had seven homers and 20 RBIs for the month. Entering August, our deficit was down to one-and-a-half games.

And still the front office sought reinforcements to the roster. Not entirely satisfied with their outfield contingent, the Giants obtained Jose Guillen from the Kansas City Royals on August 13. He immediately became the primary right fielder, starting 38 games through the end of the season. Guillen possessed a powerful throwing arm but little else, though he hit a grand slam to help us defeat Milwaukee on September 19.

The acquisition that proved to make a genuine difference occurred on August 22, when outfielder Cody Ross joined the team as a waiver pickup from the Florida Marlins. He didn't hit for a high average or a lot of power. His defense was solid but unspectacular unlike the flashy Guillen. Moreover, he never had played in the postseason. Yet while performing for four different teams in six major league seasons, Ross earned a reputation as an ideal teammate who could handle any role in any situation. Rumors about Ross' coming to the Giants began swirling a day or two before the move became official, giving Burrell ample opportunity to tell anyone who would listen, "If we get Cody Ross, we'll win the World Series."

Trailing San Diego as we did, we played a bunch of tough games in the season's second half that turned out to make a big difference in our bid to catch the Padres. In particular, four games were key.

On July 31 we were four outs away from a 1–0 loss to the Dodgers. The Giants got a reprieve when Burrell lined a full-count fastball from Jonathan Broxton over the left-field barrier with Posey aboard. The atmosphere at AT&T Park was absolutely turbocharged that afternoon. The crowd became a tad restless earlier in the eighth when Dodgers reliever Hung-Chih Kuo hit Posey with a two-out pitch. Both benches were warned against engaging in further hijinks, though given the situation, it was obvious that Posey's plunking wasn't intentional. But it did prolong the inning for Burrell. "That's why Pat's here," said Huff, Burrell's buddy. "Professional at-bats, situations like that, playoff experience, he doesn't panic and he brought that up there."

From August 23 to August 25, there was a series that never gets talked about, which mildly surprises me because I'm reminded of it when people call Oracle Park a hitters' graveyard. Granted, temperatures were higher than usual, and I recall little or no wind, but the Giants proved they could slug it out with opponents if necessary, outscoring the Cincinnati Reds 38–19 and outhitting them 53–32 while taking two out of three games. August 24 particularly stood out because big things happened up and down the batting order. Torres rapped three hits and scored four runs. Posey smacked a three-run homer. Batting 5-6-7-8, Ross, Pablo Sandoval, Uribe, and Freddy Sanchez combined to go 11-for-18 with 10 runs scored and eight driven in. Sanchez went 4-for-4.

An electrifying 2–1 win against Colorado on September 1 forever will be known as the Darren Ford game, though it had other meanings for the Giants. It meant redemption for Lincecum, who worked eight glistening innings after finishing 0–5 with a 7.82 ERA in five August starts. It meant payback for the Giants against Rockies ace Ubaldo Jimenez, who won his previous two starts against the Giants while yielding one run in 16 innings. It meant security in the division race for the Giants, who needed a win to prevent Colorado from creeping two games behind them in the NL West standings. And it meant significance for Ford, who was recalled from Double A that day. Entering the game as a pinch-runner in the eighth inning, Ford dashed to third on a wild pitch that wasn't overly wild and then charged home on catcher Miguel Olivo's throw to third. Television cameras caught Huff and Burrell punching each other in the ribs in macho glee.

The Giants simply would not have won the division title without Jonathan Sanchez, the erratic left-hander who gained consistency at exactly the right time. He won five of his last six decisions in a nine-start span, recording a 1.77 ERA, walking 26, striking out 61, and allowing 31 hits in 56 innings. If ever Sanchez was going to sag under pressure, it would have been on September 5, a nationally televised encounter against the archrival Dodgers. Sanchez yielded three hits, walked one, and struck out nine as we prevailed 3–0.

Aaron Rowand, our center fielder, put a sign above the clubhouse doors that said, "It takes 25 guys to win." Everybody would tap it on the way out. Sure enough, it seemed like we needed something from each player to get us across the finish line first. It looked bad at times. We trailed San Diego by six-and-a-half games as late as August 25. Bochy would ask me, "Hey, Murph, you want to do the lineup?"

But we rallied and went three games ahead of the Padres with three games to play at home against them. San Diego won the first two games, and now we had a real mess. You think I've got a simple job? Solving trigonometry would have been easier than considering all the possibilities for the regular season's last day. It was possible for the Giants to play three games in three cities in three days—beginning with Sunday's regular-season finale if we lost—to capture the division championship. Talk about a clubbie's nightmare! We didn't know where we were going. But if the guys did their jobs and beat San Diego in the finale, we didn't have to go anywhere. We'd capture the division title in our own ballpark. So Bochy had a meeting with the entire team after we lost on Saturday. He said, "Don't pack. We're going to win [Sunday's] game. I don't want to see any luggage or duffel bags in the clubhouse."

So I didn't put anything down. There was not a single bag in front of a single dressing stall. We went on to beat San Diego on Sunday and become division champs. I'm a firm believer in the "Nothing's over until the final out" way of thinking. But when Wilson, our closer, got two strikes on Will Venable with two outs in the ninth inning, I knew that Venable had no chance. He struck out.

The National League Division Series opener was a masterpiece. Lincecum struck out 14 Atlanta Braves in a two-hit, 1–0 victory. His strikeout total matched the highest ever recorded by a pitcher making his postseason debut. I always knew that Lincecum was capable of great things, but he absolutely outdid himself with this one. The only run was driven in by Ross, who Bochy decided to keep on the postseason roster instead of Guillen, who wasn't 100 percent physically. He might not have been 100 percent legal either. *The New York Times* reported that he had been linked to a federal investigation into shipments of performance-enhancing drugs. I don't know anything about any of that stuff. I'll leave you to make your own decisions on that.

After the NLDS switched to Atlanta with the teams tied 1–1, I received a surprise while I stepped out to watch part of Game 3 from the dugout. During a break in the action, a batboy ran over and flipped me a baseball. On it was a scribbled message:

"I thought you'd be retired by now." That was from Bobby Cox, Atlanta's manager. He had announced his plans to step down once the Braves' season ended, which happened when we won the series in four games. Hey, I know we were in the East-West tryout camp together and all that, but that didn't mean I had to quit, too.

We might not have fully realized it then, but we received a preview of coming attractions in the Game 4 NLDS finale. We won it 3–2, thanks to more Ross heroics. He homered in the sixth inning to tie the score 1–1 and lined a tiebreaking single in the seventh to account for the eventual winning run. The guy who really showed a lot of poise, though, was Bumgarner. Finishing his rookie year, Bumgarner (he dislikes being called "MadBum") worked six innings and earned the decision. It established Bumgarner's knack for postseason success, which we would see more of in the coming weeks—and years. This game also made Bumgarner—at 21 years and 72 days old—the youngest starter ever to win a postseason series clincher other than Fernando Valenzuela (20 years, 352 days) for the Dodgers in 1981.

We proceeded to Philadelphia to confront the two-time defending National League champions. Nobody gave us a chance to win the series. Then again, nobody could foresee the impact that Ross would make. Ross certainly made his presence felt during the NLDS against Atlanta by driving in three runs all in clutch situations. In all my years with the Giants, I had never seen the team make a more significant in-season player acquisition, and he wasn't done yet.

The Giants' Game 1 opponent on the mound was Roy Halladay, who no-hit Cincinnati in the NLDS. He was pitching on 10 days' rest, which is more than any non-injured pitcher would like. We countered with Lincecum, so we weren't at all intimidated. We were initially confused, though, about the wolf whistles the Philly fans made when Lincecum was on the mound. We quickly figured out that they were making fun of Lincecum's long hair, suggesting that he looked like a woman. Lincecum, though, pitched like a man. Working on eight days' rest, he struck out eight in seven innings and did well to limit Philadelphia's formidable offense to three runs.

Meanwhile, to the disbelief of observers who considered Halladay untouchable, Ross rocketed home runs to virtually the same spot in the left-field seats in the third and fifth innings. He ultimately was named Most Valuable Player of the National League Championship Series. Lopez, our left-handed specialist, did his job in the eighth inning by retiring left-handed-batting stalwarts Chase Utley and Ryan Howard. In came Wilson, and "The Beard" recorded a four-out save that preserved our 4–3 win.

Game 2 wasn't much from our perspective. Jonathan Sanchez began running out of magic dust or whatever propelled him through the regular season's final weeks, and we lost 6–1. Then, with Game 3 back at AT&T Park came a day that reminded me of all those wonderful afternoons at Seals Stadium. It was the way the sunlight hit the field. It was an absolutely golden day. The stands were packed, and the fans stayed positive from start to finish. Even before the game, it felt as if nothing could go wrong for the Giants. And nothing did. Cain started for us and pitched magnificently, allowing two hits in seven innings. Ross did his thing again, lining a two-out RBI single to open the scoring in the fourth inning. Lopez and Wilson again did the rest in the Giants' 3–0 victory. More than eight years earlier in Cain's first visit to major league spring training camp, Felipe Alou, then the Giants' manager, likened Cain to a latter-day Tom Seaver. He sure as heck looked like Seaver on this day. He clipped corners and dominated the Phillies with his fastball even when they knew he'd be throwing it. The result was a 2–1 series lead for the Giants.

Game 4 was a struggle for both sides. First the Giants controlled everything, taking a 2–0 lead through four innings behind Bumgarner. Then the Phillies sustained the outburst they were capable of, scoring four runs in the fifth inning. We responded with a run in our half of the fifth, setting up a two-run double by "The Panda." Sandoval's double gave us a 5–4 lead in the sixth, but Philly scored in the eighth inning to pull even.

Then Roy Oswalt, who won Game 2 for Philly with eight dominant innings, entered the game to pitch the ninth. I've seen enough baseball to know that no matter how good a starter is, you're placing him in an unfamiliar situation when you use him as a reliever and vice-versa. That probably was the case with Oswalt. With one out, Huff singled and advanced to third on Posey's single, his fourth hit of the game. He was the first Giants rookie to collect four hits in a postseason game since Fred Lindstrom in 1924 and the second rookie catcher to do so. Joe Garagiola, another gentleman I met while running the visiting clubhouse, preceded him, accomplishing this feat in 1946.

Up came Uribe, who was batting .095 (2-for-21) in the postseason. This was the same Uribe whose confidence typically was unshakable. This also was the same Uribe who made an excellent play on Ross Gload's grounder for the first out in the ninth inning. One way or another, you felt that Uribe would summon a winning effort from himself, and he did, launching a medium-deep fly to left field for a sacrifice fly.

With a 3–1 series edge and Lincecum starting Game 5, San Francisco couldn't help but entertain thoughts of another win that would put the Giants in their first World Series since 2002—and only the fourth of my life. But bad defense and bad luck helped the Phillies score three runs off Lincecum, who allowed only four hits in seven innings but lost 4–2. The dream was deferred.

The night before Game 6 in Philadelphia, I was at dinner and happened to be sitting near a group of Bay Area sportswriters who covered the Giants. I couldn't help but overhear their conversation. My, what a cynical group! From what I could tell, not one of them thought that the Giants could win the series. It just so happened that one of the Phillies' top scouts, a fella who all the writers knew, walked through the restaurant and stopped to chat with the writers, who repeated their bad mouthing of the Giants for his benefit. He listened for a minute, then shook his head, and smiled sadly. "You all," he said, referring to the Giants, "are outplaying us." He walked away, leaving the writers to wonder whether they weren't the faintest bit wrong.

Every pitch is meaningful in a postseason game, especially the lousy ones. Jonathan Sanchez unleashed one such pitch in the third inning of Game 6 when he hit Utley in the back with a runner on first base and the score tied 2–2. Utley disdainfully picked up the ball and flipped it toward the pitcher's mound, and most of you probably remember what happened next: a typical baseball "brawl," in which no punches were thrown yet enough hostility was generated to empty both dugouts and bullpens.

Giants bullpen coach Mark Gardner wisely grabbed Affeldt to prevent him from joining the bloodless scrum and ordered him to continue warming up. Without having to be told, Gardner reasoned that Jonathan Sanchez wouldn't be allowed to continue pitching and that the Giants would need a sharp Affeldt to enter the game. Affeldt indeed took the mound and was effective, stranding both base runners while retiring all three hitters he faced. He lengthened that streak to six by pitching a perfect fourth inning.

Affeldt looked strong enough to work another inning, but Bochy had a plan. He wanted to neutralize the Phillies with a variety of fresh arms so that nobody would tire, nobody would get overexposed, and everyone would excel. In came Bumgarner, who loaded the bases in the fifth but survived and pitched two shutout innings. Lopez needed just 12 pitches to get through a scoreless seventh.

With two outs in the eighth, Uribe hit a line drive off Ryan Madson that carried impossibly over the right-field barrier to give us a 3–2 lead. That's when I went to work. I went to the clubhouse and ordered my assistants to start chilling the champagne. Though we led by just one run, I kind of thought, *That did it right there.*

I probably should have been more cautious. Lacking more left-handers to befuddle the Phillies' lefty-heavy lineup, Bochy went to Lincecum, who you figured would blow away whoever he faced, and left the ninth inning for Wilson. But Bochy had to beckon his closer earlier than he would have liked after Lincecum allowed a pair of one-out singles. Facing Wilson, Carlos Diaz hit what initially looked like at least an RBI single. But Huff snared the ball and threw to second base for an inning-ending double play. On TV replays you can see me in the dugout, clapping my hands and cheering loudly. Heck, if we lost, I didn't want to have to get rid of all that champagne and beer.

As so often happened, Wilson made things exciting after we left the bases loaded in the ninth. Wilson grounded out to end the inning, but do you think Bochy would remove his closer for a pinch-hitter? No way. Especially not Wilson, who was going for a five-out save. He had six of them in the regular season. Wilson walked two more batters in the ninth. He ratcheted up the tension further, working the count full to Howard before slipping a 90-mph cutter past the Phillies slugger for called strike three. I was standing with the coaches in the dugout. When the final out was made, I just looked for the first couple of people to hug before going to the clubhouse and joining the happy mayhem.

I was a little nervous about facing the Texas Rangers in the World Series. Their lineup looked really formidable. Josh Hamilton seemed like a Hall of Famer-in-waiting, and the media made their ace, Cliff Lee, sound unbeatable. Bochy, who usually lets players do their own thing, must have felt the same way. He was just the tiniest bit uptight before the series began. He told the team during a meeting, "I don't want you guys showing up the other team, running out on the field just to shake a guy's hand. Just stay in the dugout."

Looking back, I think all Bochy wanted to do was emphasize a businesslike approach. It certainly worked. In each of the World Series' first two games, which were both at home, we came through with big innings that decided each contest. We took the opener 11–7 by scoring six runs in the fifth inning. And then for emphasis, we scored three more in the eighth. Lincecum didn't

Closer Brian Wilson and catcher Buster Posey embrace after Wilson saves Game 6 of the 2010 NLCS against the Philadelphia Phillies to send us to the World Series.

pitch great, but he pitched well enough to win. Freddy Sanchez rapped three doubles off Lee, who couldn't get out of the fifth inning. Nine different Giants hit safely. Seven drove in at least one run. This proved that guys were listening when Bochy said throughout the year, "Trust the man batting behind you."

We won Game 2 by the score of 9–0. It was a tight ballgame until we scored seven runs in the eighth inning with two outs and nobody on base. The biggest hit of the uprising was Edgar Renteria's two-run single, which was only fitting. Renteria called a players-only meeting by the indoor batting cage at Chicago's Wrigley Field in September, tearfully beseeching his teammates to turn up their performance a notch because the then-35 year old wanted one more crack at a World Series. I for one certainly understood how he felt and appreciated his passion.

We took our 2–0 World Series lead to Texas. "We were visitors, of course," said Bill Neukom, the Giants' managing general partner from 2009 to 2011. "But it was Murph's clubhouse. It was his from the first minute we walked across that threshold, and they were his guys."

The Rangers won 4–2 in their home in Game 3. But by now, our guys were more than sufficiently tested in big games. They weren't about to let one loss derail them. And we had Bumgarner starting Game 4. Continuing his buildup toward 2014, Bumgarner allowed three hits in eight innings in a 4–0 Giants win. The franchise's first World Series triumph since its move to San Francisco in 1958 was one win away. And we were watching the greatness of two players develop before our eyes as the Giants kept advancing.

Bumgarner walked a batter in each of the first two innings. Those were the only free passes he issued. He remained so efficient that only one Rangers batter advanced past first base, and that was partly due to third baseman Uribe's seventh-inning fielding error on a Hamilton ground ball. The fifth-youngest pitcher to start a World Series game (Bumgarner was 21 years, 91 days old on this night) performed as if he were second to none.

By homering in the eighth inning, Posey left no doubt regarding the outcome. He seemed to be maturing by the minute as he helped the pitchers through each game, most of which happened to be low-scoring. Our team ERA for the postseason was 2.47, and you could tell that Posey was mastering a catcher's various duties from blocking potential wild pitches to maintaining our staff's mental focus throughout the 15 most important games of the season.

Then came Game 5, the potential World Series finale. It was Lincecum's turn to pitch, which meant he'd be bouncing around the clubhouse, listening to Hall & Oates. (I'll give Lincecum some credit, though, because he had some appreciation for Sinatra.) He was matched up against Lee again, so we knew we'd have another challenge. But after Game 1, we knew that it was a challenge we could meet.

We sensed one thing right away: Lee wouldn't be involved in any six-run innings like he was in Game 1. He came out throwing fastballs that looked really small and breaking pitches that seemed to curl around our hitters' bats. But Lincecum matched him zero for zero, demonstrating complete command. For the longest time, it felt like nobody would score.

Then came the seventh inning.

Ross—who else?—stroked a leadoff single. Uribe also singled. Huff, a left-handed batter who would be expected to struggle against Lee, laid down a sacrifice bunt. It was a hell of a play since Huff wasn't asked to bunt very often during the regular season. Lee buckled down and struck out Burrell. Up came Renteria, who had hungered so intensely for another shot at the World Series spotlight, which he initially bathed in as a 22-year-old with the 1997 champion Marlins. Lee elevated a 2–0 pitch, and Renteria belted it over the left-center field wall. It kind of reminded me of Jim Fregosi hitting his second or third homer of the afternoon off some poor sap at Big Rec when we were kids. Well, I felt like a kid right then and there. Nine outs to go, and we would be World Series champions. But, of course, we had been here before in 2002.

This time the manager stuck with the starting pitcher. Lincecum gave up a one-out homer to Nelson Cruz in the Rangers' half of the seventh, but that was all. As usual, Wilson took over for the ninth and absolutely blew away the opposing batters, recording the final out by whiffing Cruz on a 3–2 fastball.

We went wild—just like our friends and loved ones were going wild in San Francisco. I kind of hung back, staying outside the clubhouse because I wanted this celebration to be for the players and I never liked having champagne sprayed in my face. But Neukom, the team's managing general partner, had the World Series trophy after it was presented to him on the field. He brought it to me and said, "Murph, take it in to the guys. We won it for you."

I brought it in there, but right away I gave it to Cain, who hoisted it above his head. "I definitely remember that," Cain said. "Murph was so excited! He couldn't stop smiling. He was so happy for all the guys and couldn't wait to hand off the trophy. I just happened to be the lucky one there to enjoy that moment with him. It's amazing to think about all the teams Murph has seen pass through his clubhouse and to think we somehow got to enjoy that first trophy with him. He's an amazing man."

Before that 2010 team finally won it all, I used to say, "I was at the altar three times and got knocked out three times," referring to our World Series defeats in 1962, 1989, and 2002. Well, that quote was circulated and it got the attention of some folks at ABC News. They decided to name me "Person of the Week" right after the World Series. They did a nice feature story on me about two or three minutes long that went on the air at the conclusion of their nationwide evening news telecast on November 5. They showed me sitting in my office. Bochy, Torres, and Emmanuel Burriss said nice things about me. Even my springer spaniel got some face time. The broadcaster narrating the feature called me "the father figure to the entire team." I repeated the bridesmaid comment, though I changed it to fit the occasion. This time I said, "Three times a bridesmaid, now I'm a bride."

6

Bruce Bochy

A LOT OF PEOPLE got sad when Bruce Bochy managed his final game for the Giants, but I didn't feel down at all. I knew I had gained a friend forever in Boch, who announced as spring training began that he would retire at the end of the 2019 season. As many people know, Boch has a great sense of humor. He constantly asked me to name the lineup for that day's game and relieve him of the responsibility. That in itself might not sound all that funny, but it became a running joke. And as clever as Boch can be, I thought that somehow, someway, someday, my signature would end up on the bottom of his lineup card where his usually would be, and then the joke would be on me.

Boch and I actually go way back—to 1978, when he played for the Houston Astros, and I ran the visitors' clubhouse at Candlestick Park. Boch recalled the early stages of our relationship. "He was all business," he said. "He'd talk to you a little bit, but he wanted to make sure you had everything. He was really good. He's still a tireless worker. He's still in there doing all the work he used to do. He hasn't slowed down a bit except he doesn't go on road trips."

Our friendship grew from that point, particularly after he became the Giants' manager entering the 2007 season. "He's in my office a lot," Boch said. "We sit down and talk a lot. We go back a lot of years. He knows more about baseball than people realize. He's really positive, too. 'Aaaah, we'll be all right. We'll be all right.' Murph has a way of keeping your spirits up. Now that he has scaled back on work a little bit, we spend even more time together. He'll come hang with me in my office and loves to talk baseball. He's a guy I bounce a lot of things across. He's a dear friend—not a coworker. I love that man and I'll do anything for him."

I still can't—I never will be able to—thank the Giants enough for making me the first club employee to receive his 2010 World Series ring. It was great to hear Boch endorse my selection for this honor. "Pretty cool, wasn't it? He should be the first because he had the most tenure," he said. "And I think you look at the love and respect that this man has from everybody—players, staff, front office. That was appropriate."

I was truly encouraged by the response Boch gave when a reporter asked him whether he'll miss me. "I don't plan on not seeing Murph," Boch said.

Boch already had proven capable of shaping winning ballclubs before he managed the Giants. He led the San Diego Padres to four National League titles and one World Series during his 1995–2006 tenure there. We knew he was a winner. We just didn't know how he went about the task of winning. My old friend Bud Black, who had succeeded Bochy as Padres manager, provided one explanation. "From the first pitch of a game, he has a great feel for how that game is unfolding," Black told me. "I think managers see developments…what's happening in a game that tells you what to do. Your instincts, all the innings that you've managed, there's a computer in your head that sort of tells you how to do things, and he's very good at that. It's rare that you see Bruce do something and you say, 'I wonder why he did that.' It always makes sense from my side."

Bill Virdon, Boch's first major league manager when he broke in with Houston in 1978, acknowledged that the managerial aptitude of the then-backup catcher was not immediately apparent. He didn't necessarily consider him managerial material. "I don't know that I did at that time," Virdon said. "But after I look back, I can see that he was a guy who would probably learn that. He was always straightforward, always strong, always ready, and I always liked him. He didn't have great talent, but he had good talent. He always did his job. He was always quiet, never said too much but always worked hard, was always ready to play, never questioned me."

Bob Cluck, who briefly managed Bochy in the minors, did notice Bochy's managerial acumen. "The one thing we recognized about him was that he was smart, a leader," Cluck said. "We considered him a potential coach in the major leagues."

It's often said that an effective manager rarely strays into the clubhouse because that's the players' domain. Bochy follows this unwritten rule religiously. I can tell you from my experience that whenever I'm working in the clubhouse and I hear his voice I'm immediately all ears because I figure he has something important to say. "He would leave the clubhouse to the veteran guys most of the time," said Rich Aurilia, who played for Boch in both San Diego and San Francisco. "He would never really get too involved—unless he really had to—in something going on in the clubhouse, which I think as veterans you respected out of him because it shouldn't be his job to squash every little thing that goes on. That's our responsibility."

It was no coincidence that many ballplayers had their best years with Boch managing them. Exhibit A is infielder/outfielder Phil Nevin, who endured seven professional seasons with three organizations before he blossomed under Bochy in 1999 with 24 homers and 85 RBIs. He proceeded to hit .304 with 72 homers and 233 RBIs in the 2000–01 seasons. "I really didn't have the success at this level [that] I did until I got to him," Nevin said. "But the one thing I noticed early on was he put his players in the best possible places to succeed. I felt like he was always putting you in the right spot that was best for you. I know I had been in the league for a little bit, but he gave me that opportunity in the right spots, knew the right days to give me off, when I was pinch-hitting, the right matchups. With that confidence, with success, I grew to be able to go out and have that confidence every day. I think anybody who played for him will tell you that our team was more prepared than anybody else because of him. We knew we had a chance, especially late in the game if it was close because he was better than the guy across the field. We just knew that as players. You want to win for a guy like that."

It was no coincidence that infielder Mark Loretta had his two best years under him with the Padres, batting .314 from 2003 to 2005. "He said, 'You're my everyday player.' Before that I had been an everyday player then a utility player kind of back and forth," Loretta said. "He was very quick to say, 'Hey, you're in there every day.' That freed me up a little mentally. The confidence and the steady hand that he provided me helped."

Dave Roberts batted .285 with San Diego for Bochy in 2005–06 and .257 elsewhere. Taking it a step further, including his two seasons playing in San Francisco for Bochy in 2007–08, Roberts hit .273 under Bochy and .266 in six seasons with teams not managed by him.

Roberts' regard for Bochy is genuine. Though he manages the Giants' chief rival, the Los Angeles Dodgers, Roberts bounded from the visitors' dugout to join the group of Giants paying tribute to Bochy on the field after the regular-season finale. "You create an environment where you feel that you can be yourself and perform at your highest level," Roberts said. "Boch always supported me and allowed me to be me. Boch has the ability to communicate with players, let them play, and give them that freedom because it *is* about the players. The game is always about the players. As a coach or manager, you have to understand that and put them in the best position to have success, and Boch has done that obviously for 20-plus years."

Bochy's natural leadership ability grew more pronounced as the years passed. "The meetings that he had were incredibly encouraging," said Hunter Pence, who played right field for Bochy from 2012 to 2018. "Usually, when you'd have a meeting, the manager would yell at you that you were terrible and kind of attacked you. That was all that I had known. He was one of the first managers I had who gave a pump-up speech."

Pence told me that Bochy's influence on the Giants' success was "incredible." He added, "Everything starts from the top down. Your leader sets the mark. He sets the pace and the tone and calls the shots, especially in the National League. All the baseball moves are like clockwork for him. But I think just that message in and of itself—don't be afraid to take risks, don't be afraid to fail—that really frees you up as a player."

The seeds for Bochy's biggest triumphs—the trio of World Series-winning seasons of 2010, 2012, and 2014—were planted in casual conversations with Randy Smith, son of Astros general manager Tal Smith. Intent on constructing his own winning ballclub someday, young Randy reveled in talking to players to learn more about their philosophies and what motivated them. Bochy welcomed these conversations. Smith said that he told Boch, "If I'm ever fortunate enough to become a general manager, you're the guy I'd want to manage." Smith got his wish after Padres skipper Jim Riggleman went to the Chicago Cubs prior to the 1995 season. Bochy took over as Padres manager and had them in the postseason just one year later. "To me it was one of the best decisions I ever made," Smith said.

Asked to list Bochy's personal assets as a manager, Smith cited "his knowledge of the game, his personality. He has a great feel for when to pat a guy on the back or kick them in the butt. He can defuse situations with his humor. Very good feel for pitching. To me one of the biggest differences between winning and losing is how you handle the bullpen, and I thought Bruce showed a lot of knowledge in that area."

Bochy acknowledged that maintaining relationships is essential to his job. During one of our longer chats, he told me, "Managing is managing your people. That's probably the most important aspect of the game. In-game strategy, sure, that's great. But hopefully these guys are comfortable around me. As you well know, my office is right here, and the door's always open. I do like to give them their clubhouse. I go out

Bruce Bochy holds the first of the three World Series trophies he'd win as Giants manager.

there once in a while, but it is managing your people because you're going to do things they're not going to be happy about. I don't always get it right, but I do try to communicate with them and let them know what the thinking is. At the same time, this is a spot where you have to make difficult calls, but that's your job. And your job is to put the best team out there to give you the best chance to win. I don't think that should ever change. And I don't think any relationship should ever change that. But you have to do what you need to do for what's best for the club."

Boch always seems to be able to take each player's temperature accurately at any given time. "He knew the personalities and makeup of each player every day in the room," Nevin said. This helped Boch understand how to get the most out of his roster. Giants catcher Buster Posey told me about a teammate he refused to name who threatened to be disruptive. Bochy preferred to handle the problem in a subdued manner. "Otherwise," Posey recalled Bochy saying, "he'll shut down."

Baseball experts tend to believe that Boch's Midas touch in handling the bullpen separates him from his peers. But don't expect him to conduct any clinics on the subject mainly because his procedures are unwritten and shall remain so. "I don't think there's any rules," Bochy said. "You have to adapt to your team every year, and that's including your pitching staff. The dynamic changes constantly. So I think it's up to me to adapt."

For example, Bochy constructed a bullpen that lacked set roles in 2012. Sergio Romo and Santiago Casilla divided the closer's duties. Left-handers Jeremy Affeldt and Javier Lopez might be used as lefty-on-lefty specialists or they might have joined right-handers Clay Hensley, George Kontos, or Guillermo Mota to record key outs regardless of what inning was being played. Bochy met with his relievers around midseason to discuss this. Toward the end of his address, he pointed a long finger at Affeldt and said, "In order for this to work, I need you to be on board with me." The Giants needed the versatility of Affeldt, who had proven capable of handling any role. The result was a second World Series win in three years for the Giants. Affeldt further proved his versatility in 2014, appearing in every inning from the second through 10th inning during the postseason.

Interpersonal skills also sustained Bochy from year to year. "A lot of it is his personality, his ability to get along with so many different types of people," Smith said. "That's kind of the way his career path was. He was a backup catcher, an up-and-down guy most of his career. So I think he spent a lot of time watching, listening, talking. I think he just soaked all that in, and somehow in that big head of his, it all came together, and he's become one of the greatest managers in history."

Smith emphasized that a manager's approachability cannot be underestimated: "Players have to respect who they play for, and he has to be able to communicate with them. His ability to do that with anybody—and to use humor sometimes—he can get his point across, a tough point, by injecting some humor into it. I do think that's a lost art today, a guy's ability to communicate with 30 or 35 different players, different personalities that are at different places in their careers. He's excellent at it."

A sense of continuity always seemed to link current Giants to their counterparts of bygone days. People within the organization like to call it Giants DNA. Whether Willie Mays and

Willie McCovey dominated the roster or Will Clark and Robby Thompson roamed the infield, Giants DNA was typified by the players' dedication to their craft, the passion they displayed, and an obligation to the fans to deliver their best effort day after day.

The meaning of Giants DNA seemed almost palpable during the postgame ceremonies honoring Bochy on the occasion of his imminent retirement. Because they remain essential to the organization's pride, Hall of Famers Mays, Orlando Cepeda, and Juan Marichal, as well as Felipe Alou, who has done everything possible for the organization, sat off to the side while Bochy's career was celebrated in the middle of the diamond.

The Giants organized a 72-minute program allowing current players, former players, fans, and legends to revel in the triumphs that Bochy and general manager Brian Sabean engineered. Earlier that afternoon, the participants, including 34 of Bochy's former Giants players and three ex-teammates, gathered with their significant others to socialize in an Oracle Park suite. "The room was filled with nostalgia," said outfielder Cody Ross, the Most Valuable Player of the 2010 National League Championship Series and one of the players who would take part in the ceremony honoring Bochy.

And what a ceremony it was.

The first tear-jerking event was a video tribute narrated by the soulful Tim Flannery, who is close friends with Bochy. Then came a series of Giants who, after being introduced by public-address announcer Renel Brooks-Moon, strode from the center-field gate to just behind the pitcher's mound, where Bochy awaited with handshakes and bro-hugs. First came ex-teammates

Jeffrey Leonard (Astros) and Dave Dravecky (Padres), who are now community ambassadors for the Giants. They were followed by representatives of Bochy's coaching staffs—Flannery and former pitching coach Dave Righetti.

Then came players from different segments of Bochy's 13-year managerial tenure in San Francisco. The procession began with veterans of the 2007–09 teams who won no titles but improved the roster incrementally and sustained a positive clubhouse atmosphere. Vinnie Chulk, Kevin Correia, Ryan Klesko, Brad Hennessey, Tyler Walker, Fred Lewis, Jack Taschner, Kevin Frandsen, Noah Lowry, Pedro Feliz, Ray Durham, Omar Vizquel, and Barry Bonds lined up in that order from left to right and took their symbolic bows as they entered the ballpark through the open center-field gate. A late addition to the group was Roberts, the Los Angeles manager who burst from the visitors' dugout wearing a Bochy T-shirt over his blue long-sleeved Dodgers undershirt. He also wore his Dodgers cap. Bonds playfully grabbed Roberts, lifted him off the ground, snatched his Dodgers cap, and flung it away frisbee-style.

Then came the 2010 Giants, the first of the three World Series-winning teams. Representing them (in order of introduction) were Dan Runzler, Mike Fontenot, Pat Burrell, Aubrey Huff, Andres Torres, Ross, World Series MVP Edgar Renteria, and Brian Wilson, who carried the World Series trophy.

Then came the 2012 champions. Into Oracle Park (in order of introduction) strolled Mota, Nate Schierholtz, Angel Pagan, Marco Scutaro, Barry Zito, and trophy-bearer Ryan Vogelsong, San Francisco's leading winner during that postseason when he went 3–0.

Finally, the 2014 World Series winners stepped forward. Their standard-bearers were Chris Heston, Casilla, Lopez, Gregor Blanco, Jake Peavy, and Affeldt, who had the honor of carrying the World Series trophy.

They then formed a shoulder-to-shoulder line that parted in the middle to enable one final Giants player to burst onto the field. He hadn't been here since 2015 after he sustained a hip injury that required surgery and prevented him from returning to the pitcher's mound despite repeated comeback attempts. This was his first time back to Oracle Park since being injured, and the fans let him know how much they loved and missed him by showering him with a thunderous ovation.

Welcome back, Tim Lincecum.

The two-time Cy Young award winner who gave Giants fans countless thrills during his all-too-short career was the first in this group to reach Bochy. They shared what looked for all the world like a father-and-son hug. And why not? Without each other they wouldn't be together in this hallowed place in front of thousands of fans screaming in adoration and trophies that will always sparkle.

Peavy, Blanco, Vogelsong, Posey, and Pablo Sandoval spoke individually to praise Bochy, who wore dark glasses—the better to hide his tears—throughout the program. Peavy recalled a scene that unfolded before Game 7 of the 2014 World Series: "You brought us together in a circle about as big as this mound and reminded us who we were. [You said,] 'You are all champions. You are made of champion blood.'"

Said Blanco: "Every single day I got up and said to myself, 'I just need to make my manager proud.'"

Said Vogelsong: "I know you have Kim, the boys, your daughters-in-law, the grandkids. Awesome family. But I want you to understand that all these guys back here and all the guys who aren't here, we're your family, too…You guided us probably more than you know…You gave us something that nobody can ever take from us, and that's a World Series championship."

Said Posey: "One thing that stands out for me with Boch is his tireless commitment to win, no matter what."

Said Sandoval: "It's tough for me because I call this guy my dad…To have nine years out of your 25 [as a manager] is amazing… I mentioned earlier this year that when you retire, I'll retire, but you retired too early, man. I'm sorry because I have many years left in baseball."

Then it was Bochy's turn to praise all. "I never wanted to wear out my welcome, but now I'm afraid I'm wearing out my good-bye with all this stuff that's happening here," he said.

Bochy began by thanking the consortium of Giants owners. "When I came here in 2007, I was wowed by how the ownership group trusted us and supported us on the field here because baseball is a big business," he said. "There's a lot of pressure to win, and they never wavered from giving us the resources that we needed…so I thank you for that, all the owners. They let us do our jobs without interference or questioning."

Boch then figuratively tipped his cap to Larry Baer, Giants president and CEO. "You have set a tone and created a culture here that is truly unique in baseball. Thank you for letting me be part of it," Bochy said. To director of baseball operations Farhan Zaidi, Bochy said, "I know with you this club is in good hands."

Boch then saluted those behind-the-scenes figures who never receive enough credit: his coaching staffs and the athletic trainers. "I've been blessed with an incredible staff," Boch said. "Thank you for your support because it allowed me to focus where I needed to focus on. It's been an honor to have been in the trenches with you. And Murph, that goes for you too, and all the clubhouse guys in there."

Boch proceeded to give the club's famous and talented broadcasters their due. "When I look and see why Giants baseball is so entertaining, it wouldn't be the same without Dave Flemming, Jon Miller, and, of course, Kruk and Kuip. The awards prove it, but in my heart, I *know* that they are the best broadcasting crew in baseball."

Bochy lavished Sabean with one of the warmest tributes. "When you look back upon your career, there are those pivotal moments that blow your mind," Boch said. "One of those pivotal moments for me was when Brian Sabean brought me up here to manage this club. I never thought it would be the beginning of an extraordinary collaboration and an incredible friendship. Brian, I've said this once before and I'll say it again: you are a world-class strategist, you've been a courageous buffer when I needed it and a fiery critic when I needed it. But most of all, I'm proud to call you friend. And, friend, without you I would not have experienced this great city, these great fans, and this storied franchise. I'm just grateful that we got to fight so many battles together and create so many memories together. Thank you for caring about the players, the fans, and about winning."

Boch proceeded to thank the people who make it all happen: the players. "It's no secret that you can't win championships without players—talented players who love the game and love to compete," Boch said. "I've been blessed to manage some of the best players in the game."

With many of the Giants responsible for one or more of the World Series trophies right there on display, Boch said, "You have taught me to look beyond impossible, to never say die, and never stop believing, and never, ever give up on what you're trying to accomplish. And 'torture' [referring to the unofficial mantra of the 2010 team] is better than going home."

Bochy joked about the high-wire-act pitching of Wilson and Affeldt being responsible for the two stents placed near his heart. He lauded Lincecum for "putting the fear of God in opposing hitters" despite weighing "150 pounds soaking wet." He also looked back briefly but fondly at Matt Cain's perfect game, Sandoval's three-homer binge against the Detroit Tigers in the 2012 World Series opener, and Edgar Renteria's three-run homer in the Game 5 clincher of the 2010 World Series against the Texas Rangers. "Nobody loved those Buster hugs more than me," Bochy added.

Referring to Madison Bumgarner's pitching mastery in the 2014 Series, Bochy said, "I think of watching Bum do something I don't think we'll ever see in the game again…Managing you guys has been one of the greatest joys of my life. Thank you for making me a better manager and a better person."

More emotion poured from Bochy as he paid homage to family members who were present. He called his wife, Kim, the "rock and anchor" of the family, adding that he "couldn't imagine" enduring decade after decade of baseball life without her. His voice seemed to break when he mentioned his two grandchildren, who he and Kim dote upon. "My heart is full," he said.

Bochy approached the end of his address by speaking to the fans. "We play for you," he said. "Without you there's no baseball." Bochy brought up the bitter as well as the sweet: "When I think of those years that we didn't come through for you, I apologize for disappointing you. But when I think of our championship years, I'm filled with gratitude because we did it together."

Bochy also thanked the fans for their passion. "It's difficult to put into words the impact that you've had on me personally," he said. "You guys brought so much love to this team. I can't tell you how many times we walked into this ballpark, and your energy transferred to me and these players. You made a difference here."

I can tell you that Boch was being 100 percent sincere. I recall times when he might have been dragging a little bit—maybe from an extra-inning game the night before, a cross-country flight, or just plain stress—and he'd look into the stands from his perch in the dugout, and a glow would come over his face. "Whether it was in '10, '12, or '14 or years when we were trying to get our mojo back, you've always been faithful," Bochy said. "I never took for granted or tired of leaning on that dugout rail and looking up and seeing that you packed this house. Thank you for making it such an incredible journey."

Bochy borrowed the words for his conclusion from a much more somber occasion. But they fit nonetheless: "I'll just echo the words of the great Lou Gehrig: 'I consider myself the luckiest man on the face of this Earth.'"

The Other Managers

Bruce Bochy was the 17th manager in San Francisco Giants history. Needless to say, I worked with or alongside all of them. Here's the complete list.

Bill Rigney—He was a truly nice man with a great sense of humor.

Tom Sheehan—He served as interim manager after Bill Rigney was fired in June of 1960. It was a little difficult to find a uniform that fit him since he wore size 46 pants and a 58 shirt. I'm not saying the team gave up on him, but the unofficial team slogan was "Shut up and deal."

Alvin Dark—I drove his Cadillac to spring training and back every year.

Herman Franks—He used to smoke these big cigars and leave them on top of his desk. So I'd cut off the ends and smoke them.

Clyde King—Nobody liked him. He didn't drink. He was one of those guys who'd say, "Give me a CC over [ice]." He didn't mean Canadian Club. He meant Coca-Cola! King kept to himself. Ballplayers didn't like him because he never came out of his office to talk to them.

Charlie Fox—He was very old-school. When he was in a good mood, he always sang Irish songs.

Wes Westrum—I used to kid him about how he liked to have a drink or two after the game.

Joe Altobelli—I used to say, "Joe Altobelli/He's-a-nice felli." He probably was *too* nice. He lost control of the club after they had that promising 1978 season.

Dave Bristol—He was a tough guy from the South. He wore cowboy boots, jeans, a cowboy shirt, and sometimes even a cowboy hat.

Frank Robinson—If he knew he could get to you, he'd pick on you. But if you could give it back to him, he liked it. For example, he banned food from the clubhouse during a long losing streak. Duane Kuiper and Steve Nicosia came to the clubhouse carrying lunch pails the next day to make a point.

Danny Ozark—He was the interim manager after Frank Robinson was fired.

Jim Davenport—Everybody loved Davvy, and that might have been why he lasted less than a year. Giants players relaxed under him and wouldn't play hard. It didn't help that general manager Tom Haller traded the Giants' best hitter, Jack Clark, to the St. Louis Cardinals before the season began. That denied Davvy the opportunity to come up with a formidable batting order.

Roger Craig—He was directly responsible, along with general manager Al Rosen, for the Giants' renaissance in the mid-1980s. Humm Baby! Actually, we were looking at Bob Skinner to be our manager, but he didn't want to manage. They offered him a coaching job, too, but he didn't want to be a coach. He just wanted to scout.

Dusty Baker—When he came to Candlestick Park as a rookie with the Atlanta Braves, he was just 19, but he looked even younger than that when he showed up for a late-season game in 1968. He walked into the clubhouse, and I asked him, "Can I help you?"

Baker started to say, "Well, I play for the Braves…"

"Oh, *sure* you do," I said. He looked that young! But I had to apologize when somebody grabbed Braves manager Luman Harris, who confirmed Baker's identity. We still laugh about that.

Felipe Alou—We go back to 1958, when the Giants got here. That's when he broke into the major leagues. We've remained friends ever since. When he was managing the Montreal Expos, we always got together for dinner. He's one of my three favorite managers, along with Dusty Baker and Bruce Bochy.

7

2012

I WAS JUST AS EXCITED ABOUT the 2012 season as I was in 2010, when I told anybody who would listen that we would win the World Series. We did, but the way we did it exceeded my most impossible dreams. We won six consecutive elimination games. To use tennis terminology, we fought off match point three times in a row against the Cincinnati Reds, who led the National League Division Series 2–0. Then we did it three more times against the St. Louis Cardinals, who owned a 3–1 edge in the National League Championship Series.

Throughout the regular season and into the postseason, I'd visit the coaches' locker room a few minutes before they'd head for the dugout. Tim Flannery, our musically-inclined third-base coach, would stand side-by-side with me, and we'd kick our legs as we belted out, "There's *no* business like *show* business." It was just a way to have fun while relieving some tension.

Meanwhile, the ballclub generated plenty of show business with their entertaining style of ball. Six straight win-or-go-home victories is incredible.

My initial optimism was based on old-fashioned logic. I looked up the middle. We hated to part with Andres Torres, who did so much for us in the previous three seasons. But our new center fielder, Angel Pagan, looked like he might contribute a little more to our offense due to his switch-hitting capabilities.

At shortstop we had Brandon Crawford, who looked ready to excel in his first full major league season. I'll never criticize the front office, but I know a lot of people were unhappy when veteran Orlando Cabrera was acquired at the trade deadline in 2011 to take over at shortstop for Crawford, who went to the minors. Cabrera certainly brought experience, but the critics said he didn't display anything close to Crawford's vigor. Now the Giants could benefit from Crawford's energy on a daily basis.

The biggest difference was behind the plate, where Buster Posey returned as starting catcher. He was mostly healed from the multiple left leg injuries he sustained on May 25, when Scott Cousins collided with him at home plate. Posey needed season-ending surgery, but he was mostly recovered by the time he reported to Scottsdale, Arizona, for spring training.

What fueled my optimism—*our* optimism—even further was our traditional strength: pitching. The core of our starting rotation—Madison Bumgarner, Matt Cain, Tim Lincecum, Ryan Vogelsong, and Barry Zito—looked extremely sharp.

Our biggest issue was fairly significant. We didn't really have a closer. Brian Wilson, who filled that role throughout the previous four seasons, was still battling the elbow problems that ended his 2011 season prematurely. He felt fit enough to record a save on April 12 at the Colorado Rockies before undergoing season-ending Tommy John surgery. That save was the 171st of Wilson's career. Nobody knew it then, but it also would be his last as a Giants pitcher. We had an abundance of qualified relievers, including left-handers Javier Lopez and Jeremy Affeldt and righties Santiago Casilla and Sergio Romo. But the uncertainty nagged us.

To put things mildly, the season didn't begin as we had hoped. We lost three consecutive one-run games to the Arizona Diamondbacks, who unseated us as National League West champions the year before. We proceeded to Colorado's Coors Field, that famed graveyard of pitchers. Zito was scheduled to start the first game, which looked like a difficult test for him. Injuries limited him to 13 games with the Giants in 2011. He was 43–61 with a 4.55 ERA since signing that seven-year, $126 million contract with the Giants before the 2007 season. I still believed in Zito, but I know that many of our fans had given up on him. So there was plenty of room on the bandwagon when Zito shut everybody up by pitching a four-hitter in a 7–0 triumph. He walked none, struck out four, and never allowed one of the league's most dangerous offenses to get anything going. Nobody fully knew it yet, but this was a sign of things to come—a neon sign flashing in Giants orange—for Mr. Zito.

Many teams preach about the importance of getting off to a fast start in the regular season since parity exists to some degree in every division. The Giants didn't clear .500 for good until May 18, when they beat the Oakland A's 8–6 to push their record to 20–19. We began to jell soon afterward, winning nine of 11 games from May 27 through June 7. As we began to assert ourselves as a team, left fielder Melky Cabrera, who we obtained in an offseason trade from the Kansas City Royals for Jonathan Sanchez and another left-hander, minor leaguer Ryan Verdugo, was rip-roaring hot for us. Cabrera collected 51 hits in May, tying Randy Winn's San Francisco-era (since 1958) franchise record for most hits in a month. A neat moment occurred on May 29, when he recorded his 50th hit of May to break Willie Mays' club record for that particular month. During postgame interviews that night when a reporter cited Mays in a question, Cabrera bit his lip to avoid breaking into a huge smile, even though he was speaking through an interpreter. Apparently, Willie Mays means "greatness" in any language.

If May belonged to Cabrera, then Cain was the man for June. On the 13th of the month, Cain authored the 22nd perfect game in major league history and the first ever by a Giants pitcher in a 10–0 victory against the Houston Astros at AT&T Park. Hours before the game, Cain indicated that this would be no ordinary night. A small group of professional golfers was on hand to promote the U.S. Open, which was being held that week at the Olympic Club. After finishing batting practice, Cain grabbed a driver one of the players had brought, found a golf ball, took one swing, and reached San Francisco Bay with a shot that would have been on the fairway on just about any hole at any course.

I had seen Cain dominate opponents on many occasions—but never to this extreme. He struck out two batters in each of the first eight innings except for the second and eighth innings, when he had one punchout in each. He finished with 14 strikeouts, matching Sandy Koufax's record for strikeouts in a perfect game. As somebody who was lucky enough to see Koufax pitch, I considered that fitting. On this night Cain deserved to be mentioned with the game's greats.

When Gregor Blanco made that fabulous catch on Jordan Schafer's drive to right-center field to open the seventh inning, I made sure that we were prepared for a postgame celebration. That meant chilling maybe two or three extra cases of beer. Champagne wouldn't be involved since we weren't clinching a postseason series. The most that would happen would be a beer shower for Cain. When you consider that we've had 45 United States presidents but only 22 perfect games at that time, maybe some of the bubbly stuff would have been appropriate, but I didn't want to break from tradition.

Cain retired Houston's first two batters in the ninth inning. The fans were going happily nuts with anticipation. The Astros sent up pinch-hitter Jason Castro as their 27th batter. He hit a grounder to third baseman Joaquin Arias, who backed up a step or two to field the ball. That set everybody in the dugout on edge because Arias experienced shoulder problems earlier in his career and occasionally struggled to make tough throws. But Arias guaranteed baseball immortality for Cain with a throw that was strong and true. In a book titled *One Common Goal,* which captured the story of the 2012 season, Cain recalled his perfecto as if it were "a series of freeze-frame photos." He said, "I see certain pitches leaving my hand. I see Gregor Blanco diving. I see Joaquin Arias backing up for the grounder and throwing to first for the final out of the game. I see Chelsea [Cain's wife] in the dugout afterward, crying, stunned, overwhelmed."

About a month later, Cain started for the National League in the All-Star Game and received the decision in the 8–0 victory achieved by the NL. Cain's perfect game left us three-and-a-half games behind our biggest rivals, the Los Angeles

Dodgers, in the National League West standings. As well as we were playing, we needed higher-impact players on our roster to overcome the attrition that was eating away at us. Second baseman Freddy Sanchez missed the entire season with a dislocated right shoulder that he sustained during the previous year. Third baseman Pablo Sandoval endured two stints on the disabled list; he fractured his hamate bone and then strained his left hamstring. Right knee injuries limited first baseman Aubrey Huff to 52 games.

Plus, though we didn't know it yet, Cabrera's season would end on August 15 when he tested positive for testosterone and was suspended for 50 games by Major League Baseball. Cabrera, who led the team with a .346 batting average after being named Most Valuable Player of the All-Star Game one month earlier, seemed like a huge loss. "We have to try to approach the rest of the year with a little bit of a chip on our shoulder and give everything we've got for the last 45 games," Posey told reporters.

Already, Brian Sabean had gone into overdrive to make two of the best in-season acquisitions in franchise history. He obtained second baseman Marco Scutaro from Colorado just before the July 31 trade deadline and right fielder Hunter Pence from the Philadelphia Phillies at the deadline. It reminded me of how the great New York Yankees teams of the 1950s and early '60s might struggle for a while but would end their slump by engineering a shrewd pickup. Of course, we already knew that Sabean, the major leagues' longest-tenured general manager, was more than capable of such masterstrokes.

Scutaro and Pence proved to be simply marvelous, as the saying goes. Fans initially howled at the Scutaro deal, hoping that Sabean could latch onto a big-name performer. But Scutaro immediately became a leader by example. Blessed with remarkable strike-zone awareness, Scutaro rubbed off on his free-swinging teammates by proving how being selective at the plate really can improve one's offensive production. He hit .361 and drove in 38 runs in his first 54 games as a Giants infielder. He's the reason we batted a major league-best .296 with runners in scoring position in the season's second half compared to .225 in those situations before the All-Star break.

With Pagan, Scutaro, Sandoval, and Posey batting in front of him, Pence drove in 37 runs in his first 51 games as a Giants hitter. "It's really been ridiculous," Pence said. "The at-bats I've had, base runners are everywhere. It's been incredible to see them in action."

As our leadoff hitter, Pagan often launched the action. He set a San Francisco-era (since 1958) franchise record with 15 triples, shattering the mark shared by Mays (1960) and Steve Finley (2006). Pagan also led the team with 29 stolen bases and 95 runs scored. He kept us going all year.

As I said near the beginning of this chapter, filling the closer's role concerned us at the outset of the season. But manager Bruce Bochy, who may have been the best I've ever seen at getting the matchup he wants—whether he's sending up a pinch-hitter or summoning a reliever—consistently got the most out of his bullpen. After Wilson was sidelined, Bochy initially turned to Casilla, who converted 19 of his first 21 save opportunities. Casilla eventually faltered, prompting Bochy to install the closer-by-committee format. Sharing the task of preserving ninth-inning leads is rarely associated with winning teams. But Bochy successfully used Romo, Lopez, Affeldt, and Clay Hensley to close games, relying on matchups, game situations, or even hunches to dictate who would receive that day's save opportunity. "Closer-by-committee is not an ideal thing," Lopez said. "But it's something that works for us."

It must have worked. The Giants' 94–68 record was the best of Bochy's managerial tenure in San Francisco. Also, the starters' effectiveness kept the variety of closers busy. Few of us were surprised, but everyone was impressed when the starters led a stretch of 36 consecutive shutout innings for another San Francisco-era record.

This will be remembered as the season when Bumgarner blossomed. He became the first Giants left-hander to win as many as 16 games since Kirk Rueter in 1998. Many of Bumgarner's victories proved significant. He won eight starts in games following a Giants defeat. He also affirmed his reputation as a workhorse by exceeding 200 innings for the second year in a row. Formerly of the Astros and Phillies, Pence almost sympathized with opposing hitters who struggled to make authoritative contact against Bumgarner. "I know what those hitters are up against when they're facing him," Pence said. "Standing in the outfield, I'm kind of laughing because I know what they're dealing with."

Vogelsong further entrenched himself in the rotation by sustaining durability few pitchers could match. He lasted six innings or more in his first 21 starts, a streak matched at the time only by Washington Nationals pitcher Jordan Zimmermann. Considered a novelty one year earlier because of his surprise rise from obscurity to the National League All-Star team, Vogelsong kept striving to prove that he was legitimately talented. "I never did anything close to good at the major league level until last year," he said. "I heard all the questions in the offseason of whether it was a fluke and could I do it again."

Zito hushed the skeptics, who derided him for his big contract, by recording his first winning record (13–8) as a Giants pitcher. A combination of circumstances helped him thrive. The previous December he married the former Amber Marie Seyer, which brought him stability he never knew. "It just seems like there's a counterbalance now to all the intensity and focus that's required on the field," he said. "There's something to come home to. There's something more important than baseball. And now, I feel like I have some perspective."

During my dugout visits when Zito pitched, I could tell that he had refined his repertoire of deliveries. "There's less of that floating change-up. It's a little more sharp," pitching coach Dave Righetti said. "The curveball's not as big. It's a little tighter and easier for him to get it over the plate and in the strike zone."

No longer possessing the overpowering fastball that helped him win the National League Cy Young award in 2008 and '09, Lincecum lost a career-high 15 games and slipped from his perch among the league's top pitchers. One day I heard him making fun of himself by calling himself a "thumber," which was short for "cunny thumber." That's the label applied to pitchers who rely on off-speed stuff such as curves and change-ups because they can't throw hard. I wasn't having any of that, so I scolded him. "You're not a thumber! And you never will be!" He just gave me a sad smile. But Lincecum was too good to be kept down for long. His season wasn't a failure. As October would prove, it was quite the opposite.

As always, good defense accompanied good pitching. Crawford overcame an early-season rash of errors to establish himself as a magician at shortstop. He committed 12 errors in his first 59 games but was charged with just three miscues in his next 78 appearances. Crawford made difficult short-hop grounders look routine. He displayed considerable range to either side and regularly showed off the most powerful throwing arm of any homegrown Giants shortstop since the heyday of three-time All-Star Chris Speier in the 1970s. Now you know why I issued him Speier's No. 35.

Cain spoke for each pitcher when he praised the club's defense. "These guys have done a great job all year for me, picking me up and making spectacular plays behind me," Cain said. "As a pitcher that motivates you to keep wanting to go back out there to pitch well. You've got guys behind you who are pushing to win games any way they can, putting their bodies on the line. That's always an effort you appreciate as a pitcher."

Posey delivered the season's supreme effort, joining the list of all-time Giants greats by winning the National League Most Valuable Player award. Showing no ill effects from his unspeakable injury, Posey hit .336 with 24 home runs and 103 RBIs. He also captured the Hank Aaron award as the NL's top all-around hitter, won the Silver Slugger award as the league's most prolific offensive catcher, and was elected NL Comeback Player of the Year.

Posey always has been sincerely humble. "The awards I ended up winning at the end of the season belonged to the whole organization," he said. "It's easier to shine as a player when you have a strong ownership group and front-office staff that put guys on the field who love the game and want to win, when you have great teammates who make it fun to come to the ballpark every day, when you have experienced and responsive coaches, and when you have smart and devoted fans who make every game feel like the World Series."

We wore down the rest of the NL West with our midseason upgrades. We finished eight games ahead of the second-place Dodgers. But we actually looked a bit listless in the NLDS opener against the Reds, who won 5–2. We looked even worse in Game 2, mustering two hits in a 9–0 defeat. To make matters worse, both games were at home. Being down two games to none in a best-of-five series, we should have had little or no chance to turn things around in our favor, especially since the Reds hadn't lost three home games in a row all year.

What happened in Cincinnati was very simple. Corny as it sounds, our guys refused to give up. Before the game Bochy stood before the team and gave an inspiring address, citing great postseason comebacks and the Old Testament story of Gideon's army, a band of 300 Israelites who defeated a Midianite army exceeding 100,000. It was an excellent motivational talk. In fact, it might have been one of the very best motivational speeches I've heard, and being a clubhouse manager, I've heard a lot of them.

Then Pence got up and poured out his heart and guts in his now-famous speech, which trumped Bochy's. "I'm going to give absolutely everything I have for one more day because I love playing with you guys," was one of his main points. The guys left the clubhouse feeling immortal.

But Reds starter Homer Bailey had a way of evaporating all that enthusiasm. He no-hit the Pittsburgh Pirates about two weeks before this game and would no-hit the Giants the following season. On this day he struck out our 3–4–5 hitters, Sandoval, Posey, and Pence, in the first two innings. We were down 1–0 by that point, and it could have been worse. Facing Vogelsong, Brandon Phillips stroked a leadoff single, stole second base, and headed for third when Vogelsong's pitch eluded Posey. But our savvy catcher pounced on the ball and managed to throw out Phillips. That ended the Reds' chance for a big inning.

We scored in the third inning without the benefit of a hit. Bailey hit Blanco and walked Crawford before Vogelsong's sacrifice bunt and Pagan's sacrifice fly pushed across the tying run. We were still deadlocked 1–1 after nine innings. Scutaro's sixth-inning single was our lone hit. At least, though, Bailey was out of the game. Instead, Jonathan Broxton was pitching for the Reds, which ought to have given the Giants—and our fans—a jolt of confidence. Sure, Broxton had a good arm and all that, but most of our hitters felt comfortable in the batter's box against him from having faced him dozens of times when he was a Dodgers reliever. His ERA against us exceeded 4.00 at the time.

Sure enough, Posey and Pence singled. Broxton recovered nicely, striking out Brandon Belt and Xavier Nady. But Broxton's first pitch to Arias deflected off the glove of catcher Ryan Hanigan. After the runners advanced, Arias hit a grounder that might have skipped a little bit on third baseman Scott Rolen, who dropped the ball. Rolen recovered it quickly and threw to first base, but the bobble was enough to allow Arias to reach first base safely, which scored Posey. Romo pitched a perfect 10th to seal the victory, which sustained the spirit of Pence and might have tickled the baseball gods. After all, Hanigan was guilty of three passed balls all season, and Rolen was an eight-time Gold Glove recipient. So the Giants won because a guy who rarely commits passed balls committed a passed ball, and another guy, who usually avoids errors, made an error.

There was much less drama in Game 4, which the Giants won 8–3 to even the series. Only the seventh team since 1900 to reach the postseason while finishing last in the majors in home runs, the Giants outslugged the Reds as Pagan, Blanco, and Sandoval homered. Seven of their 11 hits went for extra bases, including four doubles. But the game's most notable aspect might have been pitching. Zito couldn't survive the third inning, but Lincecum compensated with his longest relief outing of the postseason. He lasted four-and-a-third innings and allowed two hits and one run while walking none and striking out six. He threw an amazing 42 strikes in 55 pitches.

The Giants knew they would find the Reds at their best in the Game 5 series finale. San Francisco faced a familiar foe: right-hander Mat Latos, with whom they clashed in several intense confrontations when he pitched for the San Diego Padres. Performing as an MVP should, Posey whacked a grand slam to fuel a six-run, fifth-inning outburst that broke a scoreless tie. But the Reds eroded the lead, which stood at 6–3 entering the ninth inning.

I felt fairly calm because Romo is the consummate strike-thrower. But he walked Zack Cozart with one out. Joey Votto and Ryan Ludwick singled, scoring Cozart and bringing the potential winning run to the plate in the form of Jay Bruce, an All-Star that season. Bruce fouled off five 1–2 pitches and worked the count to 3–2 before lifting a harmless fly ball to left field. Rolen struck out to end the series, granting Pence and his teammates what they wanted: more time together.

We didn't immediately know who we would play in the National League Championship Series. Washington and St. Louis had to finish duking it out in the other National League Division Series before we knew whether we'd head home to play St. Louis or go to Washington to oppose the Nationals. It looked like we'd make another trip to our nation's capital when Washington entered the ninth inning with a 7–5 lead. But while we were waiting inside our plane on the airport runway, the Cardinals scored four ninth-inning runs to win the game and their series. The way they won was instructive. Two of their lesser-known players, Daniel Descalso and Pete Kozma, each hit two-out, two-run singles to account for the scoring. We knew that we'd have to scrap harder than we did against Cincinnati to get by St. Louis. And if you could call any team a postseason rival of ours, it was the Cardinals. They beat us in a seven-game NLCS in 1987 that didn't exactly feature the best of manners. Jeffrey Leonard annoyed the Cardinals with his "one flap down" home-run trot, and Chili Davis angered Missourians everywhere by calling St. Louis a "cowtown." In 2002 Kenny Lofton chirped a little too much for the Cardinals' tastes as well.

There was more in store for 2012. After a relatively uneventful Game 1, which St. Louis won 6–4, Game 2 began with Cardinals slugger Matt Holliday sliding hard into second baseman Scutaro in a first-inning attempt to break up a double play. This did not lead to any open animosity between the clubs. But some observers and many fans believed that the 6'4, 240-pound" Holliday was unnecessarily rough on the 5'10", 185-pound Scutaro.

The Giants evened the series with a 7–1 triumph in that game. Then St. Louis took command, winning Game 3 and Game 4 to take a 3–1 lead in the series. Game 3 was especially frustrating for the Giants, who rapped nine hits but couldn't sustain any offense. That was indicated by our 11 runners left on base and 0-for-7 hitting with runners in scoring position. Game 4 was no better. Bochy started Lincecum, which made sense given the right-hander's effectiveness as a reliever. Perhaps, Bochy thought Lincecum had found himself. The four runs and six hits Lincecum yielded in four-and-two-thirds innings suggested otherwise.

This trend would continue in Game 5, the experts insisted. Zito looked below average in his NLDS start at Cincinnati, and so some thought that his regular-season luck had run out. But the skeptics had no idea what Zito was about. Because of his more balanced outlook on pitching and life, Zito could more easily embrace a challenge like this instead of letting it overwhelm him.

All of the momentum was on the Cardinals' side. And Zito took all of it for himself and the Giants on this Friday night in St. Louis. He bent it in San Francisco's direction with the force of his will. When he was done dominating the Cardinals through seven-and-two-thirds innings in the Giants' 5–0 triumph, it was clear who would win this series. And it wouldn't be the Cardinals, though they still clung to a 3–2 series lead.

Zito's mound opponent, Lance Lynn, initially appeared destined to follow the script for this game that most people had written. He struck out the side in the second inning, following a perfect first. Then came the Cardinals' turn to bat and some early trouble for Zito. Yadier Molina singled to lead off the inning and chugged to third base on David Freese's double. Descalso was up next, and Zito struck him out, intentionally walked Kozma, and coaxed Lynn's inning-ending, double-play grounder.

Zito would not self-destruct on this night as he had in other games. That misfortune was reserved for Lynn. One out after Scutaro and Sandoval singled to open the fourth inning, Pence tapped a comebacker to Lynn, who threw to second base in an attempt to record a force-out or perhaps even start an inning-ending double play. But Lynn literally threw to second base. The ball skipped off the bag and out of reach, enabling Scutaro to score the first run. Blanco drew a two-out walk to load the bases for Crawford, who singled to drive in two runs. Up came Zito, an indifferent hitter at best. His bunt up the third-base line resulted in another single that delivered Blanco and concluded the Giants' four-run uprising.

Meanwhile, Zito never faltered. He yielded six hits and walked just one. "You could see that from the beginning on he had that aura around him," Cain said. But Bochy opted to remain cautious. Once Zito threw his season-high 115th pitch, which Carlos Beltran popped up to left field, Bochy unlocked the bullpen door and summoned Casilla, who fanned Holliday and stranded a runner. Appearing in a non-save situation, Romo blanked the Cardinals in the ninth. The pair of righties preserved Zito's outstanding effort.

Asked about Zito's pitching renaissance overall, Cain said, "It shows what kind of class he has as a person, as a teammate, and as a friend. And then it showed his professionalism. He never stopped trying to find ways to get better throughout the years that he struggled. And throughout all the criticism and everything, he kept fighting and trying to find ways to do things different."

Other Giants were content to do things the same. With the series having returned to San Francisco, they maintained pressure on the Cardinals in Game 6 with a 6–1 victory that evened the series. The Giants led 5–0 after two innings, which plainly reflected the respective moods of each team. Vogelsong demonstrated that he was prepared to challenge the Cardinals by throwing 12 consecutive fastballs to open the game. "It's not unusual for me to do that sometimes," said Vogelsong, who struck out a career-high nine batters in seven innings while allowing four hits and St. Louis' lone run. "I just kind of saw the way our team reacted the other night when Barry came out and kind of took the bull by the horns and was throwing up zeroes. I saw how our team was feeding off of that. And I just knew that I had to go out there and keep [the Cardinals] off the board early and give us a chance to do something offensively."

Scutaro did the most. He rapped a pair of hits in three at-bats, including a two-run double that contributed to San Francisco's four-run second inning. That prompted the humorous postgame question, "Can you explain why Matt Holliday sliding into you made you a better hitter?" Replied Scutaro, who must not have felt like showing off his understated sense of humor, "I'm just happy to be here in this situation."

Not much changed in Game 7, which was the last of the elimination games the Giants faced in this postseason. Again they jumped to a commanding early lead. This time it was 7–0 through three innings. Again they benefited from a big inning, as Pence's bases-loaded, three-run double highlighted a five-run third inning. Again they received solid pitching, as Cain worked the first five-and-two-thirds innings of the Giants'

9–0 triumph that advanced them to the World Series for the second time in three years. Just before he left the game, Cain opened the sixth inning by plunking Holliday squarely on the butt just to remind him what the Giants thought of his slide into Scutaro.

The last couple of innings were played in heavy showers. A euphoric Scutaro tilted his head back and opened his mouth wide. Let it rain, let it rain, let it rain! And shortly before the final out, I saw the daughter of Harmon and Sue Burns, who were major investors in the Giants. I told her, "This isn't rain. It's your mother in heaven crying tears of joy."

We weren't supposed to win the World Series either. In fact, we were the underdog in each postseason series we played in 2010, 2012, and 2014. Conventional wisdom dictated that Justin Verlander, the Game 1 starter for our World Series opponent, the Detroit Tigers, was poised to jam our bats down our throats. A lot of people considered him the best right-hander in the major leagues, and that indeed may have been true. In the years following this World Series, Verlander's career has remained on a Hall of Fame trajectory. I hope he makes it.

His plaque at Cooperstown won't say anything about how Sandoval humbled him on Wednesday, October 24, the night the 2012 World Series began. The Panda belted three homers in the Giants' 8–3 victory. I've seen Sandoval play some fantastic games, but this went far beyond anything he has done—before or since—on a baseball field. The first two homers came off Verlander, who allowed five runs and six hits in four innings. Sandoval hit his third of the night off Al Albuquerque. It was the fifth three-homer game in the 108-year existence of the World

Pablo Sandoval rounds the bases after hitting a two-run home run during the third inning of Game 1 of the 2012 World Series.

Series, duplicating Babe Ruth (twice), Reggie Jackson, and Albert Pujols. You might say that Sandoval awakened memories of Pujols' presence, Jackson's flair for the dramatic, and…Ruth's tummy.

Panda provided support for Zito, who started in 14 consecutive Giants victories—11 in the regular season and three in the postseason. Zito personally compiled a 9–0 record with a 3.46 ERA in this stretch. Our other pitching star in this game was Lincecum, who worked two-and-a-third innings of hitless relief. Even though he didn't start, he generated plenty of excitement from our crowd when he jogged to the bullpen to warm up. It reminded me of a basketball game when a great sixth man leaves the bench and creates a buzz just by heading for the scorer's table.

Game 2 the next night was much more tense. We had to make an outstanding defensive play in the second inning to deny Detroit a run. Bumgarner hit Detroit's Prince Fielder with a pitch to open the inning. Delmon Young followed with what appeared to be an RBI double. But quick, accurate relays from left fielder Blanco and Scutaro, who ranged far from his position at second base to function as a second cutoff man (shortstop Crawford also was aligned to possibly take a throw), enabled Posey to tag Fielder on the sole of his right shoe.

Nobody scored until the seventh when we loaded the bases on Pence's single, Brandon Belt's walk, and Blanco's bunt single that died a little less than halfway up the third-base line. Crawford grounded into a double play that enabled Pence to score. We added a run in the eighth without benefit of a hit, as a trio of walks set up Pence's sacrifice fly. Romo retired the Tigers 1–2–3 in the ninth. Give a lot of credit to Bumgarner, who allowed just two hits in seven innings after what had been a rough postseason for him (10 earned runs and 15 hits allowed in eight innings spanning two starts).

I couldn't celebrate openly because we hadn't won anything yet. But as we prepared to travel to Detroit, I felt pretty good about my preseason prediction of another World Series title.

We experienced an inconvenience upon arriving in Detroit. Due partly to existing accommodation shortages and partly because the Detroit Lions had a home game on Sunday (the World Series would resume with Game 3 on Saturday), our traveling party had to stay in four separate hotels! We were spread out among the Somerset Inn, a boutique hotel called the Townsend, the Westin Cadillac downtown, and a place in suburban Dearborn. But we came together when it counted most.

Vogelsong—"Vogey" to most of us—started Game 3. He had allowed only one run in each of his previous three games during this postseason. However, obviously enough, this would be his first World Series appearance. But all of us knew that he wouldn't wilt under the pressure. Vogey's too tough for that. Just as obviously, it was fair to wonder whether the Tigers, who had such a formidable offense, would wake up as a result of playing at home.

Forget it.

Gametime temperature for Game 3 at Comerica Park was 47 degrees, a little cooler than we were accustomed to. But that didn't bother us. We didn't do much with the bats against the very tough Anibal Sanchez—Blanco tripled home Pence and scored on Crawford's two-out single in the second inning—but Detroit did even less. That's because Vogelsong concentrated with every fiber of his being to hold the Tigers scoreless for five-and-two-thirds innings. I realize that sounds terribly corny, but it's true. He issued four walks mainly because he was pitching so intently and refused to give in to any of Detroit's hitters. Vogey left the game after walking Andy Dirks. In came Lincecum. He got Jhonny Peralta to fly out to Pence in right field. Lincecum proceeded to carve out what was virtually a duplicate of his Game 1 performance. Continuing to throw pitches that had more late movement than he perhaps had ever displayed, he no-hit the Tigers for two-and-a-third more innings. He walked one and struck out three, improving his postseason statistics to 1–0 with an 0.69 ERA in five games. In 13 innings he allowed one earned run and three hits while issuing two walks and throwing 17 strikeouts.

Romo pitched another perfect ninth, leaving us one win away from another World Series title. The Tigers had been shut out twice all season. Now we had blanked them two games in a row. As confident as we were, we wondered how long we could maintain our mastery of their hitters. But with Cain starting Game 4, why not?

As it turned out, Cain went out there with less than his best stuff. That sort of thing tends to happen when you've pitched 242 ⅓ innings, but as he proved many times, Cain at less than 100 percent was a heck of a lot better than most guys at the top of their game.

The temperature was even colder for Game 4. It was 45 degrees when Detroit's Max Scherzer threw the first pitch. Then the inevitable happened. Detroit's Miguel Cabrera, who had two singles in nine at-bats and one RBI in the first three World Series games after leading the majors with 44 home runs and 139 RBIs during the regular season, socked a two-run homer in the third inning to put Detroit on top 2–1. It was the first time the Tigers led throughout the entire series.

Cain settled down, and in the sixth inning, Posey slapped a two-run homer to put us back on top. But the Tigers responded with a run in their half of the inning on Young's two-out homer. That tied the score and ultimately forced extra innings since the Giants mustered one single, and Detroit went hitless in the final three innings.

Our designated hitter for the evening, Ryan Theriot, singled to christen the 10th inning. Theriot became virtually a forgotten man once Scutaro joined the club. But he came up big when it counted most. Crawford, a left-handed batter, overcame the challenge of facing a left-handed pitcher, Phil Coke, and laid down an effective sacrifice bunt to advance Theriot to second base. Coke struck out Pagan. Up came Scutaro, facing the situation that he mastered so frequently since joining the Giants: batting with a man in scoring position. Looking back on it, the Tigers probably should have intentionally walked Scutaro. Maybe they didn't because Sandoval, who had crushed them in Game 1, was on deck. Anyway, Scutaro did what you'd expect him to do. He singled cleanly to right-center field, giving us a 4–3 lead.

In came Romo for the 10th. Back in spring training of 2010, Wilson said: "An elite closer is the guy who gets the final out of the World Series." I guess that makes good old Sergio an elite closer. He fanned Austin Jackson and Don Kelly before freezing Cabrera with a batting-practice-speed fastball.

We were champions again! The postgame celebration was beyond great, of course. It was maybe a little less emotional because the 2010 conquest meant *so* much to a franchise that hadn't captured a World Series title since 1954, but the champagne tasted just as sweet. And celebrating with the guys was just as meaningful.

8

Nicknames and Numbers

IDEALLY, A NICKNAME is both exclusive and inclusive. It's exclusive because it belongs solely to the player who receives it, and it's inclusive because a good nickname helps a player feel like one of the guys. Coming up with nicknames was one of my unofficial duties when I was the Giants' clubhouse manager—and even before that when I was Eddie Logan's assistant. None of these names were remotely vulgar. We were just trying to have a little fun.

I hate to say it, but I think the art of creating nicknames is lost. Too often what we see these days is adding "er" to a person's last name or shortening a player's first and/or last names. Thus, the Giants had "Cainer" for Matt Cain and "Madbum" for Madison Bumgarner. With all due fairness to today's younger players, those aren't nicknames. They're derivatives. They would not have passed muster in bygone decades. Here's a partial list of the nicknames linked with Giants players. I came up with most but not all of these.

Jeremy Affeldt—"Aflac"
This was because his last name and the insurance company's name sound alike. In this case, however, it's also suitable because Jeremy

Affeldt, who loves to talk, could drown out a flock of geese, the insurance company's mascots, in a matter of seconds.

Matty Alou—"Mousie"
He was a little tiny guy (5'9", 160 pounds) who ran as if he was a mouse. Among the great Alou brothers, he probably was the fastest. But even with all that speed, he didn't dare try to score on Willie Mays' two-out double in the ninth inning of Game 7 of the 1962 World Series. He almost surely would have been thrown out at home plate. Matty Alou couldn't break into the Giants' starting outfield, but think about what a clutch performer he was in that '62 season. His leadoff single in the ninth inning of that World Series Game 7 gave the Giants hope. He also singled to launch their game-winning, four-run uprising in the ninth inning of the National League playoff finale against the Los Angeles Dodgers.

Mike Aldrete—"Mario"
Mike Aldrete took this one to the major leagues with him from Stanford University, where he attended college. It was reasoned that his surname sounded enough like that of auto racing legend Mario Andretti to make the moniker stick. I also called him "Scaldo" because he scalded so many line drives as a hitter.

Joe Amalfitano—"Louie" "The Italian Guy" "Buddy Guy"
To me "Amalfitano" is not difficult to pronounce. But several people, including Horace Stoneham, struggled with it. So a lot of guys called him "Louie" for no particular reason other than it was much easier to say than "Amalfitano." And, like a lot of

baseball-related humor, it made no sense at all. Mr. Stoneham called him "The Italian Guy." Though I never had trouble with his name, I simplified things further by calling him "Buddy Guy."

Joaquin Arias—"Captain Phillips"
Have you ever seen the movie, *Captain Phillips*? If you have, think about the bad guy who took over the ship. Joaquin Arias looks just like him! It's funny because in real life Arias probably wouldn't even jaywalk. He's extremely mild-mannered. And let me remind you: we might not have won the 2012 division title without him. He filled in at third base while Pablo Sandoval was injured and hit .417 with 15 RBIs in 24 games during August. We didn't skip a beat.

Rich Aurilia—"Goomba"
This refers to Richie Aurilia's Italian heritage. I understand that it can be meant as a derogatory term. Obviously, I never felt negatively about Aurilia, who I love like a son.

Rod Beck—"Shooter"
According to clubhouse legend, Rod Beck had a minor league teammate who called everybody "Big Shooter" likely because he struggled to remember names. But in Beck's case, the name stuck.

Marvin Benard—"Marvelous Marv"
I should give my apologies on this one to New York Mets first baseman Marv Throneberry, who received that nickname when he regularly performed on-field comedy with the hapless 1962 New York Mets.

Bud Black—"Tijuana Harry"
Bud Black lived in San Diego near Tijuana, Mexico. His real first name is Harry (not Harold). Throw it all in the nickname machine, and this is what you get.

Gregor Blanco—"Blanquito"
I couldn't help but use the diminutive form of Gregor Blanco's last name. Generously listed at 5'10", he made so many big plays and got so many key hits for us during our 2012 and 2014 World Series-winning seasons.

Bobby Bonds—"Booscaloosa"
Bobby Bonds came from southern California, but he liked to talk about the deep south a lot. So I gave him a southern-sounding nickname. I know it's silly and makes no sense at all, but that's part of the fun of nicknames. It was fun watching him play, too. What remarkable talent he had. His abundance of five-tool skills (hitting for average, hitting for power, speed, fielding, and throwing) was exceeded probably only by Willie Mays.

Ron Bryant—"The Bear"
Obviously, it's a partial spinoff from the legendary college football coach, Paul "Bear" Bryant, but Ron Bryant took the nickname seriously. He carried this big stuffed bear everywhere for good luck. It even had its own seat on flights. National League hitters had to bear down particularly hard against Bryant in 1973, when he led the league with 24 wins. But he was injured in a swimming pool accident the following spring and finished 1974 with a 3–15 record.

Pat Burrell—"Irish"

There's some ethnic profiling here, but I'm half-Irish myself, so I felt comfortable stamping this label on "Pat the Bat." To tell you the truth, I'm not even sure he's Irish, but he always seemed responsive when I used this nickname for him.

Matt Cain—"Bam Bam"

This one *didn't* stick. I don't know why. I thought it was fitting. Remember Bam Bam, the toddler, who appeared in various episodes of *The Flintstones* cartoon series? When Matt Cain was called up to the Giants in 2005, he made his major league debut when he was still a month shy of turning 21. He had a rookie's inexperience and a man's physical gifts, which he ultimately took advantage of during the 2010 and 2012 postseasons.

Will Clark—"Nuschler"

Nuschler (pronounced NOOSH-ler) is Will Clark's real middle name. People called him "Noosh" for short. And when he stared with that white-hot intense expression, that was referred to as his "Nuschler face." Clark received a lot of teasing from the guys, especially in his first couple of big league seasons, but he'd get so fired up about baseball that he probably needed to calm down just a little. Poking fun at him might have been necessary to help turn his competitive fire down a notch so the club could get the most out of him.

Brandon Crawford—"Crawfish"

I used a little wordplay here. Brandon Crawford's so quiet that he hasn't used a nickname for me yet, but he's so clever that he probably has come up with something and is waiting for the right time to use it.

Matt Cain, the pitcher who I jokingly called "Bam Bam," developed into an ace who threw a perfect game on June 13, 2012.

Jimmy Davenport—"Goofus" "Peanut"
Jimmy Davenport liked to play jokes on people, which led to "Goofus" because he had this goofy side to him. "Peanut" came from his height or lack of it at 5'11", but I never thought of him as undersized. His mastery of infield defense made him a towering figure in my estimation.

Darrell Evans—"Hoover" "Doody"
The first nickname refers to Darrell Evans' fielding excellence. Like a Hoover vacuum, he seemed to pick up everything hit in his direction. He was a vastly underrated third baseman. "Doody" came from his resemblance to the children's TV puppet show character, "Howdy Doody." When Willie McCovey hit ahead or behind Evans in the batting order, he motivated his teammate by saying, "You and me, Doody?" More than 20 years later, McCovey would greet Evans wherever they crossed paths by flashing his big smile and repeating, "You and me, Doody?"

Mike Felder—"Tiny"
The 5'8", 160-pound Mike Felder had arguably the best two seasons of his 10-year career with the Giants, batting .275 for them in 1991–92 and .239 for his three other teams.

Kevin Frandsen—"Franny Farkel"
This is another nickname, which is based on pure silliness. He'd respond by calling me "Papa Smurf" or "Murph the Surf." It was like our little inside joke.

Tito Fuentes—"Sweetback"
I came up with this one after watching the friendly way he dealt with people, especially the ladies.

Alan Gallagher—"Dirty Al"
Every game Alan Gallagher did something—slide, dive for a ball, collide with another player—that soiled his uniform. I identified strongly with Dirty Al, who was the first native San Franciscan to play for the Giants.

Ed Halicki—"Ho-Ho"
Ed Halicki stood 6'7". Well, the TV commercials for Green Giant vegetables featured a skyscraper-sized person who exclaimed, "Ho, ho, ho." Since Halicki was as tall as a giant, this became his nickname. I'll remember the afternoon of August 24, 1975, forever. That's the day Halicki no-hit the New York Mets in a 6–0 victory at Candlestick Park in the second game of a doubleheader. This was when I worked the visitors' clubhouse, so I had to temper my enthusiasm quite a bit.

Ken Henderson—"Skitch"
This nickname was derived from Skitch Henderson, the original bandleader for NBC's *The Tonight Show*. Sometimes we'd add onto it by calling him "Skitchee-skoo."

Glenallen Hill—"Space Ghost"
Glenallen Hill was a good, solid ballplayer, but sometimes before games he'd walk around the clubhouse while appearing to be staring off into space.

Marc Hill—"Boot"
You have to be of a certain age to understand this one. (For that matter, you have to be of a certain age to understand some of these other nicknames, too.) Boot Hill is the name of an unspecified number of cemeteries, mostly in the western United States. It was a common name for the burial grounds of gunfighters or those who "died with their boots on."

Derek Holland—"Holland America"
If you like to take big, fancy vacations, you'll know what I'm talking about. Holland America is a highly regarded cruise line that spans the globe.

Dave Kingman—"King Kong"
This nickname seemed fitting once we saw Dave Kingman hit. True, he struck out way too much, but he also hit home runs that had to be seen to be believed. When he played for the Chicago Cubs, his homers regularly cleared not only the left-field bleachers, but also crossed the street. At Candlestick Park I saw him hit the scoreboard with a homer off Atlanta Braves pitcher Buzz Capra, and that scoreboard stood probably 80 to 100 feet beyond the left-field wall. We might have held onto him, but we couldn't find a position that he could play adequately. The designated hitter position in the American League was made for him.

Bill Laskey—"Tree"
One look at him and you'd understand. He stands 6'5", and his heart is as big as he is. He once was quoted as saying, "I hate the

Dodgers. I hate 'em, I hate 'em, I hate 'em." If you're a Giants fan, you've got to love that, love that, love that.

Gary Lavelle—"Pudge"
Gary Lavelle was a great relief pitcher for us through 11 seasons (1974–84). If he pitched today, he'd probably be even better given the way relievers are used. But Lavelle, whose 647 career appearances remain a franchise record, had a little bit of a stomach on him.

Jeffrey Leonard—"Hac-Man"
Most of you surely are familiar with this one. This combines Jeffrey Leonard's free-swinging tendencies with early-era video-game culture.

Bob Lillis—"Flea"
Slender at 5'11" and 160 pounds, Bob Lillis seemed to dart like a bug around the infield during his playing days. That led to his nickname.

Bill Madlock—"Puppy's Feet"
The perennial .300 hitter could have shopped for shoes at the children's department. He wore a size-6 shoe if you can believe that.

Juan Marichal—"Popeye"
This nickname is a sign of respect. Juan Marichal excelled so consistently that he almost seemed to be a comic book or kid's TV hero like Popeye. I used to tell him, "The way you were throwing, you must have had your spinach this morning." With his

incomparable leg kick, his control, his mound presence, there'll never be another like him.

Kirt Manwaring—"Man-O-War"
The spelling of Kirt Manwaring's last name lent itself to this nickname. Plus, like the champion thoroughbred, Manwaring was pretty darned tough. He proved that by averaging 108 games caught per year from 1992 to 1996.

Greg Minton—"Moon Man"
Most of Greg Minton's offbeat behavior was hidden from the public. Trust me, the man was different, but he was all business on the mound, racking up 19 saves or more in every season from 1980 to 1984.

John Montefusco—"The Count"
With that drop-and-drive delivery of his, John Montefusco looked like Count Dracula swooping in on a hitter. I told him that he should wear a cape out to the mound.

Joe Panik—"Don't Panic"
I used to say this to Joe Panik just as he'd leave the clubhouse for the start of a game—not that I was worried about Panik ever actually panicking. He was about as cool and level-headed as they come.

Phil Ouellette—"Omelet"
He appeared in 10 games in 1986, and that was it for his major league career. If he had been around more, there might have been quite a few hungry Giants. He had quite the appetite.

Gaylord Perry—"The Greaser"

Publicly, Gaylord Perry never has admitted to throwing doctored baseballs. But many hitters who faced Perry, whose autobiography was titled *Me And The Spitter*, have no doubt that he did, and he never complained about the nickname I gave him. Though he spent less than half of his major league career with the Giants (10 years in 22 seasons), I'm glad that the ballclub recognized his achievements by having a statue built in his honor, along with the other San Francisco-era Hall of Famers.

Bill Posedel—"Porthole"

Bill Posedel was a pitching coach who liked to talk about the Navy a lot. So I had to come up with something maritime-related for him. The alliteration helped the nickname stick.

Rick Reuschel—"Big Daddy"

Figuring this one out is simple. Rick Reuschel carried what was about 240 pounds on a 6'3" frame. The right-hander was as big in status as he was in stature, posting a 36–19 record from 1988 to 1989.

Dave Righetti—"Magoo"

He loved his pitchers, which came naturally since he was the pitching coach. But he worried so much about them. Sometimes a Giants pitcher would throw a crucial pitch, and Dave Righetti would look away. Then he'd look at you and ask, "What happened? Did he get a hit?"

I'd say, "Jesus Christ! You sound like Mr. Magoo!" That was the television cartoon character who'd fret a lot. So I started calling him "Magoo."

Kirk Rueter—"Woody"
This nickname alludes to Kirk Reuter's resemblance to the cowboy character voiced by Tom Hanks in the animated movie *Toy Story*. Reuter gave fans plenty of time to learn his nickname, lasting 10 years in the starting rotation while becoming the second left-hander in the Giants' San Francisco history to win 100 games.

Dave Roberts—"Doc"
This is because of his initials. I don't wish any of the Los Angeles Dodgers success, but I kind of make an exception with him. It's safe to say that he's absolutely one of the nicest people in the big leagues.

Hector Sanchez—"George Clooney"
Despite the obvious ethnic differences, if you take just a quick glance at Hector Sanchez, you'll see the resemblance.

Denard Span—"Spic-and-Span"
If he was a big RBI guy, we would say he cleans off runners from the bases. He was still injured when he arrived here, so he had to work hard just to get ready to play. Denard Span, though, never complained or made excuses.

Eli Whiteside—"Whitey"
This was *not* a pun on his surname. He earned this nickname with his prematurely gray-turning-white hair. He had a full head of it, too.

Matt Williams—"The Big Marine"
When Matt Williams played for the Giants, he had close-cropped hair, almost balding. That, as well as his impressive build, helped give him a militaristic look. He certainly was as intense as any marine. Sometimes after an 0-for-4 game, he'd throw stuff around and shake up the clubhouse.

Trevor Wilson—"Bobcat"
At the beginning of his career, Trevor Wilson couldn't accomplish much with the great stuff he had because he was so wild. Wilson was as wild as this wildcat.

Wes Westrum—"Nappy"
Wes Westrum never liked to admit that he might have been out having a few drinks after a game. If you mentioned seeing him at the bar the night before, he'd say, "Who, me? I wasn't at the bar." I'd come back with, "You must have been napping then because I talked to you!"

By The Numbers
Like a nickname, a player's jersey number can become a player's identity. What longtime Giants fan doesn't associate 24 with Willie Mays? What percentage of New York Yankees fans see the No. 7 and instantly think of Mickey Mantle? So we don't just grab a jersey from a hanger and hand it over to the next ballplayer in line. For instance, consider the year (2005) when we took reliever Robb Nen's No. 31 out of circulation. That was a tribute to a man who gave everything to the team's effort to win, even though he knew he was further injuring himself and

hastening the end of his career by continuing to pitch. If it were up to me, nobody would wear No. 31 again. I think Nen belongs in the Hall of Fame.

As this is being written, we haven't issued No. 55 since Tim Lincecum stopped pitching for us in 2015. We used a record number of players last year and we still didn't give it to anyone. That's not out of blind, undying loyalty to Lincecum, but also think of the pressure that would be placed on some innocent rookie if we gave him No. 55. Now that a little more time has passed, 2020 could be the year that we take No. 55 out of mothballs.

There are certain numbers that we'd prefer not to issue to just anybody, such as 35. Three All-Star shortstops have worn that number—Chris Speier (1971–77, 1987–89), Rich Aurilia (1995–2003, 2007–09), and Brandon Crawford (2011–present), and we'd like to keep it that way as much as possible. Of course, no ballclub perpetually has an All-Star shortstop on its roster, so multiple players who don't match the profiles of Speier, Aurilia, and Crawford probably will wear No. 35 in the next decade or two.

Speier has derived personal and spiritual significance from No. 35. "Three stands for my God, my family, and the blessing of playing baseball as a profession," he said. "Five was going to stand for the number of children we were going to have, and I messed that up by having six. Passing it down to Richie and Brandon… it means a lot to me that they want to wear it. I hope Brandon wears it for a long, long time."

Another number that we don't want to give to just anybody is 12. That was the number Jim Davenport wore throughout his Giants tenure, which began with the team's inaugural San

Francisco season in 1958 and ended in 1970. He continued to serve the Giants in various roles until his death in 2016 at age 82. To longtime Giants fans, Davenport meant as much to the team as Mays, Willie McCovey, or Juan Marichal. He embodied stability on the field with his solid defense and clutch hitting, as well as class off the field and gentlemanly behavior. Numerous Giants wore No. 12 after Davenport retired from playing—the most notable ones included Gary Thomasson, Nate Schierholtz, and manager Dusty Baker, who wore 12 throughout his playing career—but I never found anyone who fit Davenport's image until second baseman Joe Panik broke into the major leagues in 2014. Heck, I was ready to button Panik's jersey for him. I was overjoyed that the Davenport family felt the same way. Davenport's son, Gary, was quoted as saying, "Murph doesn't just kind of haphazardly give out numbers. He wouldn't give Dad's number to anybody. To give it to Joe, I couldn't have picked a better person. Joe's very similar to Dad. He's got a lot of fire in him, he goes about his business, he's really quiet about it, he's just a grinder."

More numbers have a story behind them than you might think. For example, only a handful of Giants have worn a number higher than the No. 70 that hung from the shoulders of right-hander George Kontos from 2012 to 2017. Kontos came to San Francisco from the Yankees, who have retired an unusually large batch of numbers due to their preponderance of great players. When the Yankees summoned Kontos for his major league debut in September 2011, he found a jersey adorned with the No. 70 hanging in his dressing stall. "I was just grateful to have a major league uniform with a number on the back of it," he said. As Kontos told me later, he liked wearing a "round number." Moreover, his mother reminded him that No. 7 is lucky (and that her birthday is November 7). That explains his eagerness to wear No. 70 with the Giants, though I told him that we had lower numbers available. Virtually every Giants number has a backstory. Here are some of the others:

1—I don't know whether power influences get preference, but three managers have worn this number with San Francisco: Alvin Dark, Dave Bristol, and Jim Davenport, who likely gave up No. 12 so Dusty Baker, who was in his 17th year as a player, could continue to wear it.

2—The first five players to wear this number were catchers. Of course, "2" is the designation for catcher when scoring games. Eddie Logan either believed in stating the obvious or wanted to make things easier for official scorers.

6—It's rare that two players in a row wearing the same number carve out distinguished careers for themselves. It happened for the Giants with second baseman Robby Thompson (1986–96) and first baseman J.T. Snow (1997–2005).

13—The Giants must have been a superstitious bunch. Not until the team's 26th season in San Francisco did a Giants player dare to wear this number. Left-hander Mark Davis didn't seem to mind. He pitched impressively until he was traded to the San Diego Padres in 1987. He won the National League Cy Young award two years later.

15—Here's yet another example of Bruce Bochy's intelligence and ability to handle people. At the 2011 trade deadline, the Giants acquired outfielder Carlos Beltran, who wanted to continue wearing his beloved No. 15. That was the same number Bochy had worn since 1983. Wanting to keep the club's prized pickup happy, Bochy yielded No. 15 to Beltran and took 16. Bochy insisted on nothing in return, but the gracious Beltran gave him a Panerai wristwatch. Bochy soon got his number back when Beltran signed with the St. Louis Cardinals as a free agent. But with that nice watch, you could say that Bochy came out ahead.

19—Here's another example of a numbers switch but with more emotion behind it. Infielder Kevin Frandsen was drafted by the Giants in 2004 and assigned to the organization's short-season Class A Salem-Keizer affiliate. Through sheer chance he was issued No. 19, the favorite number of his brother, DJ, who was fighting cancer. DJ adored Dave Righetti, who wore 19 as a reliever with the Yankees and Giants and continued to wear it as the Giants' pitching coach. Righetti knew the Frandsen family well, having grown up with the boys' father. After battling cancer for 19 years, DJ died later in '04 at age 25. Two years later the Giants promoted Frandsen to the majors. He initially wore No. 8. Shortly after his recall, though, he found No. 19 in his locker. Righetti had engineered the whole thing. "He knows how much it means to you," I told Frandsen.

20—Frank Robinson wore this number when he took over as manager in 1981. One year after Robinson's dismissal during the 1984 season, Jeffrey Leonard began wearing it as a tribute to him. He continued to wear it through the 1987 season. The Giants eventually retired it in honor of Hall of Fame outfielder Monte Irvin.

22—This number will be retired during 2020 in honor of Will Clark, whose career appeared to be on a Hall of Fame trajectory through six seasons. Many fans also will link No. 22 to Jack Clark, who hit .277 with 163 homers and from 1975 to 1984.

24—Really, does anything need to be said? Willie Mays made this number synonymous with baseball greatness. Mays actually wore No. 14 at the outset of his big league career before switching to the number he immortalized.

25—Barry Bonds obviously has made No. 25 his. The Giants retired it in his honor in 2018. But, similar to the Will and Jack Clark situation with No. 22, Bobby Bonds, Barry's father, performed some memorable feats of his own while wearing No. 25 (186 homers, 263 stolen bases with San Francisco from 1968 to 1974).

40—I had a good feeling when we issued this number to Madison Bumgarner back in 2009. Another left-hander, Mike McCormick, wore it in 1967 when he became the first Giants pitcher to win the Cy Young award.

44—Willie McCovey asked for this number because he wanted to emulate Braves slugger Hank Aaron, a fellow Mobile, Alabama, native. McCovey eventually developed his own following.

All those years I spent running the visiting clubhouse came rushing back to me when I served as the Giants' representative, along with Ryan Vogelsong, at the 2018 MLB Draft telecast. There, representing the Atlanta Braves, were Dale Murphy and Ralph Garr. Rollie Fingers, who I met when he played for the San Diego Padres, was there on behalf of the Oakland A's.

Ryan Vogelsong and I were the representatives for the Giants at the 2018 Major League Baseball Draft. It was quite a thrill. (Getty Images)

Murphy developed into probably the best player in baseball by the early 1980s. He won back-to-back Most Valuable Player awards in 1982–83. I certainly saw the best of him; he tied Willie Stargell for the most home runs hit by a visiting player with 25 apiece. In trying to beat Murphy, pitchers beat themselves by throwing Murphy outside. But instead of avoiding his power—as pitchers logically thought they were doing—they actually were playing into his hands, as well as wrists, forearms, and such. Murphy loved to drive the ball to right-center field, a skill that especially worked well at Candlestick Park, where a jet stream often blew in that direction. That added to Murphy's propulsion. So many of Murphy's Candlestick homers left the yard via right-center.

Something else about Murph—I guess I can call him that, right?—he belongs in the Hall of Fame. Maybe he fell short statistically (.265 career batting average, 398 homers). But if you can keep Pete Rose out of the Hall of Fame because of his bad behavior, then a guy like Murphy should receive some consideration for doing something every day like signing autographs, answering fan mail, making a personal appearance to make the game better. But his fate is in the hands of the Veteran's Committee, and they don't let too many guys in.

One of the fastest guys I've seen from home plate to first base, Garr still looks like he could make an infielder rush a throw. Fingers was as carefree as ever. We're on national TV and supposed to be behaving ourselves, but Fingers was sitting behind me tossing wads of paper at the back of my head. Let's just say he still has good control.

I don't just think about the star players. I think about the staff. I still think a lot about Alexis Busch, our batgirl who died in a sailing accident in April 2012. Busch was the first full-time batgirl in the major leagues, but that's not why she sticks out in my mind. She always focused on her job, worked hard, and kept a positive attitude. She always showed up at the ballpark already in uniform, demonstrating her passion for the game. "She really just thought of herself as another girl who loved baseball," said her father Corey Busch, the team's executive vice president for 13 years.

She saw a lot of exciting baseball—much of it generated by Barry Bonds. She was the lone person to greet Bonds at home plate when he hit his 500th home run. She picked up his bat and offered a fist bump. She also witnessed much of Bonds' chase for the all-time single-season home run mark in 2001. Bonds rewrote the record book by hitting 73 homers. Fittingly, Bonds spoke at the memorial service honoring her, which was held at the ballpark. "Alexis made us feel at ease," Bonds said.

Also, the Giants dedicated a plaque to her and placed it adjacent to the bat rack in their dugout. I've been lucky enough to maintain a lifetime career in baseball. It all began by being a batboy at Seals Stadium. Busch and I had the same beginning. Thus, I identified closely with Busch and her love of the game. I've continued to remember her and keep her in my thoughts and prayers.

9

2014

The crowd at the Kansas City Royals' Kauffman Stadium was cheering louder and louder by the second, though nothing was happening. But a lot was about to happen, which explained all the noise. Anticipation will do that.

The situation that generated so much excitement was one of the classic dramas that only sports can create so spontaneously. The bottom of the ninth inning of Game 7 of the World Series was about to begin. The Giants led the Royals 3–2, and Madison Bumgarner was ready to head for the mound to pitch his fifth inning of relief. He was performing on only two days' rest after pitching a four-hit shutout in Game 5 of the World Series. I usually don't say much when I watch a game from the dugout, but I was wondering the same thing that millions of others following the World Series had on their minds. "Hey, Boch," I said, trying to sound as conversational as I could and avoid editorial comment. "Is Bum going to pitch the ninth?"

I could tell from the briefest of glares Bruce Bochy shot me that I wasn't going to get away with this one. He said with barely veiled contempt, "Oh, another manager, huh?"

Of course, we hugged it out later. Bochy wasn't truly angry with me, but the magnitude of the moment left him a bit tense, as you might guess. He didn't need any comments from the peanut gallery to cast doubt on his moves at this moment. Besides, who could criticize Bochy for sticking with Bumgarner for as long as he could? Bum already had rewritten the record books with his postseason performance. He was absolutely the right man for the job, which happened to be silencing Kansas City's offense to deliver us a World Series triumph.

Bumgarner entered the ninth inning having retired 12 consecutive batters. He lengthened that streak to 14 by striking out Eric Hosmer and retiring Billy Butler on a foul pop-up. That left Alex Gordon, who lined out against Bumgarner to end the sixth inning. Gordon also had accounted for all of Kansas City's scoring, having doubled home a run before coming around to score in the second inning.

This time Gordon hit a ball to left-center field that looked for just a moment like it would be the final out. Gregor Blanco's mind was changing, too. Unfortunately, he was playing center field, and I was in street clothes in the dugout. My indecision was harmless; his wasn't. He charged the hit late and slipped slightly, enabling the ball to get by him. Left fielder Juan Perez tracked the ball down and dropped it when he initially tried to pick it up. By then, Gordon had decided to remain at third base. Due up was Salvador Perez, who owned a .348 World Series batting average. The crowd roared nonstop. Bumgarner had to be exhausted. Somehow he found the strength to force Perez to hit another lazy foul pop-up, and this one headed toward third base. Pablo Sandoval made his famous catch-it-and-kneel-in-gratitude move, sealing the Giants' third World Series title in five years. I'm telling you, the champagne tasted as good as it did the first time.

Around the middle of that game, Michael Morse, the most overlooked clutch hitter in Giants history, approached me. I call him overlooked because it seems like he never got enough credit for what he did for us during that postseason. His eighth-inning homer in Game 5 of the National League Championship Series against the St. Louis Cardinals tied the score and set up Travis Ishikawa's big home run. On this night he was essential, driving in two of our three runs with a sacrifice fly and a single. Anyway, Morse had something to tell me. "If I get the car," he said, "I'm giving it to you."

He meant the car that the Most Valuable Player of the World Series receives. The way Bumgarner was pitching, I didn't think Morse had a shot. But it was nice of him to think of me.

Did you know that I had a hand in saving that game for the Giants? Okay, maybe I didn't quite save it. I did, however, prevent what could have been an awkward delay. Many of us recall second baseman Joe Panik's third-inning diving stop of Hosmer's sharp ground ball up the middle, which started a 4-6-3 double play and stopped a Royals rally before it began. Panik ruined his belt buckle while diving for the ball. I quickly offered him my belt, and he accepted. He changed into a new belt between innings. Shoot, if I knew what I know now, I would have fished Panik's belt from whatever trash can it was thrown into and saved it for Cooperstown!

It was that kind of season for the Giants, too. They needed quick fixes and changes to stay in the postseason hunt. And in the end, they came about as close as any club ever to rely on a single-handed effort while winning a World Series.

The pitchers, who once led them, had faded from prominence. Tim Lincecum really hadn't been the same since 2001, but he was so good that he still could win games at a decent rate even with diminished stuff. Heck, he no-hit the San Diego Padres for the second season in a row in 2014. But he could not dominate hitters as constantly as he once did. Bochy sent him to the bullpen in August. His 12–9 record actually looked decent; the same could not be said about his 4.74 ERA.

At least Lincecum could pitch. Injuries had nagged Matt Cain since 2013. Three trips to the disabled list limited Cain to 15 starts this year. He went 2–7 with a 4.18 ERA. His 2014 season ended on August 11 when he underwent surgery to remove bone chips from his right (throwing) elbow. In typically tough Cain fashion, he learned in 2010 that the chips existed, but he still continued to pitch. Both opened the season in the starting rotation, which was strengthened by free-agent acquisition Tim Hudson. I don't know where we would have been in the National League West standings without him. He was 38 to start the season but pitched as if he were 28. He won seven of his first nine decisions while compiling a 1.81 ERA. He lasted at least seven innings in each of his first seven starts and in 10 of 13. It was not a stretch to consider him a Cy Young award candidate.

Ryan Vogelsong was our fifth starter. Occasionally, we'd skip his turn in the rotation, but we still saw flashes of the guy who was our leading winner in the 2012 postseason. Keeping him in the rotation was not an issue.

Then there was Bumgarner.

He was in the midst of a stretch (2013–16) where he seemed destined to become a first-ballot Hall of Famer. He made the All-Star team and finished among the top 10 in Cy Young Award voting each of those four years. He also won two Silver Slugger awards for his prowess at the plate. I have never seen another Giants pitcher who loved to hit as much as Bumgarner. In fact, there are very few people who love to do anything as much as Bumgarner. He simply throws himself into everything he does. No pun intended. "It's a mind-set of whether you want to push yourself to do everything you can do and do whatever it takes to get there, or whether you don't and want to cut corners," Bumgarner said in a 2016 issue of *Giants Magazine*. "I don't know exactly where it comes from, but it's nothing more than a mind-set. I want to do everything I can do to be as good as I can be, and that's it. I don't think it's an option to cut corners. If it's going to be beneficial for you, your career, and your family, how can you not do it just because you don't want to put in the time and effort?"

What we had started to see in the last year or so was steadier behavior from Bum. Oh, he'd still get angry at times and he'd vent his frustrations with opponents at times. But overall, he seemed to understand that losing control of his emotions was counterproductive to his No. 1 goal of winning. He found ways to express his emotions without letting them get the best of him. "Early in my career, I would let my thoughts and feelings carry past the moment," he said. "It would stay with me the next inning or next couple of innings, and I'd be mentally stuck two or three innings ago. The next thing you know, the game's out of hand, it's a lopsided score, and you don't know what happened. For me, the more time you spend trying to hold in your emotions, the tougher it makes it. It's easier to be aware of your emotions, let them go, and move on."

Many other Giants must have followed Bumgarner's example. Because at one juncture, they looked "stuck," as he would say. As a result, they had to qualify for the postseason as a wild-card team. The Giants weren't thinking wild-card for most of the season. Their 43–21 record on June 8 was the National League's best and gave them a comfortable 10-game lead over the second-place Los Angeles Dodgers in the division standings.

Then the narrative shifted sharply from: "How do these guys ever lose?" to "How do these jokers ever win?" The Giants lost 41 of their next 67 games, including 18 of 23 in a 25-day span to fall behind the Dodgers into second place in the National League West. San Francisco virtually forgot how to win at home, where its record was a woeful 7–22 from June 9 to August 12. The Giants never occupied first place after July 26 and had to close with a 19–12 rush just to secure a wild-card postseason berth.

It was tough. Every team endures injuries, but I maintain that we had more than our share. First baseman Brandon Belt missed 96 games with a broken left thumb and a concussion. Morse, my would-be auto supplier, was out for almost all of September with a left oblique strain. Center fielder Angel Pagan missed 57 games with back inflammation before undergoing season-ending surgery to repair a bulging disc in his back. Backup catcher Hector Sanchez missed 58 games with a concussion. And second baseman Marco Scutaro was sidelined for nearly the entire season with a lower back strain.

Fortunately, we received a boost from two unexpected sources: rookies Panik and Andrew Susac. Panik ranked fourth in the NL with a .338 batting average from August 1 to the end of the season while Susac, a catcher, batted .273 with three home runs and 19 RBIs in 35 games. Yusmeiro Petit established a major league record by retiring 46 consecutive batters in a stretch of eight appearances from July 22 to August 28. The right-hander's finest moment, however, was awaiting him in the postseason.

We needed a useful stretch-drive acquisition to bolster our sagging starting pitching. We got it in the form of Jake Peavy, Bochy's ace when both were with San Diego. I must admit that some of us were a little skeptical about Peavy since he came from the Boston Red Sox with a 1–9 record. What the disbelievers forgot was that Peavy had stamped himself as a proven winner long ago. He lost his first three starts with the Giants, but then he won six of seven decisions in a nine-game stretch. All but one were quality outings. His ERA in this nine-start span was 1.35. I'd say he knew how to pitch. He definitely knew how to win.

One other thing about Peavy's arrival in San Francisco was that he got the clubhouse stereo going again during the pregame dressing period. He usually played The Grateful Dead when he pitched. Peavy's a musician himself and has performed at many shows and benefits. I'll stick to Frank Sinatra, but at least he favored a group that has a San Francisco influence.

We beat San Diego three out of four times to end the regular season, but we didn't need that to feel good about ourselves heading into the wild-card game at Pittsburgh. We had Madison Bumgarner starting for us against the Pirates. I was idly chatting with one of our advance scouts, who followed the Pirates for about a week to 10 days to familiarize himself (and eventually the ballclub) with their tendencies. He had acquired a healthy respect for the Pirates, maybe a little too healthy. "This team has power," the scout said as we watched the Pirates finish batting practice. "They're a lineup with pop from leadoff to the No. 8 spot in the order. They're smart defensively and they really have good throwing arms. I'd say the starting lineup has 'plus' arms at nearly every position. Edinson Volquez can throw just about every pitch for a strike. When he's on, he's awfully tough."

Gee whiz, who were we playing: the 2014 Pittsburgh Pirates or the 1927 New York Yankees? I excused myself before I let the scout convince me that the Giants had absolutely no chance against the Pirates.

Our scout should have visited the PNC Park grandstands to deliver his report. Then again, it might have sounded repetitive to these rabid fans. The ferocity of the cheers from the good citizens of Pittsburgh and its environs told me that they fully expected the Pirates to win. To further whip up fan frenzy, the Pirates called for a "blackout," requesting each spectator to wear a black T-shirt, top, or blouse to demonstrate their unanimity.

This admirable display of team spirit didn't survive the fourth inning. The game was scoreless through three innings. Then we loaded the bases on singles by Sandoval and Hunter Pence and a walk to Belt. Up came Brandon Crawford, the NL's fifth-best hitter in September with a .365 batting average. It was October 1, but Crawford apparently didn't change his calendar. He lifted a hanging curveball into the right-field seats. Man, that crowd quieted down in a hurry. I'm not criticizing their fans, but in the same situation, our fans would have kept on yelling, trying to spark a rally. The Pittsburgh folks just flat-out gave up. That made it even easier for us to cruise to an 8–0 victory, our seventh straight in a win-or-go-home game. In fairness, Bumgarner gave them nothing to holler about. He allowed four hits, walked one, and struck out 10 in a complete-game effort, becoming the third pitcher in history to record double-digit strikeouts in an elimination game. Sandy Koufax and Justin Verlander were the others. Thus began the Giants' 25th trip to the postseason in franchise history. It was on to Washington for the National League Division Series.

We won the opener against the Nationals 3–2. Though it was a close game, it wasn't especially pressure-packed unless Hunter Strickland was in for us. We led 3–0 entering the bottom of the seventh when Strickland, as he tends to do, gave up home runs. He allowed one to his nemesis, Bryce Harper, and the other to Asdrubal Cabrera. Strick has excellent velocity. His pitches, however, lack great movement. That's why hitters can get around on his fastball and drive it a long way.

By the time the 2019 postseason rolled around, nothing had changed for Strickland. Facing the Dodgers in the Division Series for Washington, interestingly enough, Strickland allowed three home runs in two games over a two-inning span. That left him with nine homers allowed (out of 14 hits) in 13 innings covering 13 appearances. Now, I'm not much when it comes to analyzing statistics, but I look at these figures and I wonder why anybody would trust Strickland in the late innings. It's a cold but fairly simple conclusion to reach.

No use in making you wait to recap what happened in Game 2 in 2014. After all, both teams made you wait long enough that night. We won it 2–1 on a home run by Belt in the 18th inning. It tied the record for longest postseason game in terms of innings and set a new standard for longest game in terms of duration—six hours and 23 minutes. In the era of baseball that was played when I was a Giants batboy, you could play three games in that amount of time. I'm not exaggerating.

The Nationals very well could have won this game in nine innings. Nats starter Jordan Zimmermann looked unbeatable, nursing a 1–0 lead and a three-hitter into the ninth inning. Panik showed superb poise for a rookie by drawing a two-out walk that prolonged the game. Zimmermann didn't look like he was weakening at all, but Matt Williams, our old friend who was managing the Nats, decided to summon his closer, Drew Storen. It's difficult to criticize Williams in this instance because closers are for situations like this. Unfortunately for the Nats, the strategy didn't work. Panik went to second base on Buster Posey's single and scored on Sandoval's double. Posey was thrown out at home on the play. That would be the closest either team came to scoring for quite some time.

Bochy brought in Petit, who set that regular-season record for consecutive batters retired, to open the 12th. Petit spared Boch the burden of having to think too much about his pitching. He lasted *six* innings! He basically handcuffed the Nats by allowing one hit during his stint. That's the value of having a long reliever, somebody who's accustomed to starting. He can handle these multiple-inning stints with relative ease.

But we still had to score a run. Juan Perez walked and advanced on a sacrifice bunt in the 11th inning, and Pence doubled to christen the 12th, but nothing came of those mild opportunities. In the 17th inning Williams' choice of pitchers was right-hander Tanner Roark, who ideally would be the Nats' version of Petit. Roark was a starter by trade, having crafted a handsome 15–10 record with a 2.85 ERA in 31 games that season. He pitched a perfect 17th, and nothing seemed amiss when he worked the count full on Belt to open the 18th inning. Then *pow.* Belt unleashed that buggy-whip swing of his to golf Roark's delivery into the right-field upper deck. The clock struck 11:35 PM immediately after Belt made contact.

Belt, who was 0-for-6 in this game entering his final at-bat, acknowledged that he had to try to force himself to ignore his futility. "It was tough at times," he said. "That was something I had to kind of figure out before the last at-bat. I knew I wasn't having great at-bats the entire game. I wasn't sticking with the plan that I had in the previous five or six games. I had to restart a little bit. Just get a good at-bat, and whatever happens, happens."

Belt's homer put the Giants in good position to advance to the National League Championship Series. In major league history, teams leading a best-of-five series 2–0 advanced to the next step on 62 of 70 occasions. Further helping the Giants was the change in venue from Washington to San Francisco.

With Bumgarner starting Game 3 against Washington's Doug Fister, the smart money, so to speak, was on the Giants to lengthen their 10-game postseason winning streak, which matched the third longest in big league history. Once again, pitching dominated the action, as the teams played to a scoreless tie through six innings, but Asdrubal Cabrera's RBI single sealed Washington's 3–1 triumph.

To nobody's surprise, offense was virtually nonexistent in Game 4. The Giants left 10 runners on base and went 1-for-11 with runners in scoring position. Yet they prevailed 3–2 partly because Washington performed a tad loosely on defense, as it had done in Game 3. Washington starter Gio Gonzalez's poor throw to second base on an attempted force-out and Vogelsong's bunt single helped the Giants load the bases with one out in the second inning. They scored twice on Blanco's walk and Panik's ground-out.

That was anything but dynamic. But the Giants limited the Nats to four hits while relying on Vogelsong, who permitted one run and two hits in five and two-thirds innings, and righty relievers Sergio Romo and Santiago Casilla, who contributed a shutout inning apiece. The Giants' 3–2 win put them in the NLCS against the Cardinals for the fourth time since divisional play began in 1969. Their most recent meeting occurred in 2012, when the Giants overcame a 3–1 series deficit by winning a crucial Game 5 in St. Louis behind Barry Zito before capturing the final two games by the combined score of 15–1.

Each NLCS confrontation against the Cardinals left a lingering taste among Giants fans. The first mouthful was bitter; the succeeding ones were oh, so sweet.

In 1987 the Giants and their fans were thrilled to be involved in the postseason again for the first time since 1971. The series began with the fuss surrounding Jeffrey Leonard's "one flap down" home-run trot, which angered the Cardinals. St. Louis right-hander Bob Forsch hit Leonard with a pitch in Game 3 to notify him that his base-running style wasn't appreciated. This didn't stop Leonard from homering for the fourth straight game the next day. Giants outfielder Chili Davis' slighting reference to St. Louis as a "cow town" also led to some hard feelings among Cardinals fans, which soared after they overcame a 3–2 series deficit to win it in seven games. The Giants didn't score a single run in the final two games at St. Louis, though Leonard still finished with a 1.417 OPS to earn series MVP honors.

In 2002 the Giants ended this series in the relatively brief span of five games, but it probably felt like a seven-game series to many fans and even some participants because the final three games were being decided by one run. Home runs by Mike Matheny, Jim Edmonds, and Eli Marrero, who broke a 4–4 tie in the sixth inning, offset Barry Bonds' three-run homer in the fifth inning and lifted the Cardinals to a 5–4 victory, which trimmed the Giants' edge in the series to 2–1. The next day, the Giants amassed just four hits but made them count as NLCS MVP Benito Santiago smacked a two-run, eighth-inning homer that propelled the Giants to a 4–3 triumph, which left them one victory away from the World Series. Then in Game 5, Kenny Lofton's two-out, ninth-inning single scored David Bell, whose spread-eagled slide home borders on iconic, to break a 1–1 tie and give the Giants a 2–1 win.

In the 2012 NLCS, the Giants were trailing in the series 3–1 but won three consecutive elimination games to advance to their second World Series in three years. Zito, the oft-criticized left-hander, continued silencing his critics by working seven-and-two-thirds innings in Game 5 at St. Louis as the Giants prevailed 5–0. This victory signaled a complete turnaround in fortunes.

This brings us back to 2014 and the unusual combination of circumstances that produced the next Giants-Cardinals NLCS hero: Ishikawa, who very easily could have been drowning in dejection at this juncture instead of basking in jubilation. He generated the enduring joy with a tiebreaking three-run homer in the ninth inning of Game 5 that gave the Giants a 6–3 victory and punched their tickets to the World Series.

Released by five organizations since 2011, Ishikawa was on the verge of quitting baseball in June of 2014. He was sick of being away from his family and tired of his mediocre performance on the field. Ishikawa, who had spent parts of four seasons with the Giants and won a World Series ring with them in 2010, was batting .260 for the Giants' Triple A Fresno affiliate and sensed that no improvement was imminent. Recalling that dark period, he told me, "If they put the ball on a tee, I'd swing and miss."

After a game in Round Rock, Texas, while performing for the Giants' Triple A Fresno affiliate, the Grizzlies, in late June, he telephoned his wife, Rochelle, and his best friend, Danny Graham. As he told various reporters, he shared his fears about his baseball future to Rochelle. Having been drafted by the Giants out of high school, Ishikawa had no immediate career options outside of baseball. He consulted his Bible for comfort. But as he said, "My mind was so cluttered. I might as well have been reading Chinese or Spanish."

Pacing through the hotel parking lot, Ishikawa then called Graham, his pitching coach at Federal Way (Washington) High School who had evolved into a confidant and was the best man at his wedding. Ishikawa wept into the phone while swatting at Texas-sized beetles and poured out his heart for an hour and a half. In return, Graham offered encouragement and cited Romans 8:35: "Who shall separate us from the love of Christ?"

"He felt like he let everybody down," Graham said. "The one thing I wanted to convey to him was, 'Travis, no matter what happens, I'm going to love you. I don't love you for what you do. I love you for who you are. Worst-case scenario: if you never play baseball again, we're still going to be best friends. That being said, you're a persevering guy.'"

Soothed by Graham's support, Ishikawa again telephoned Rochelle to share reassurance. After initially questioning the hardship he endured, Ishikawa currently regards it as part of the journey he had to travel before reaching the pinnacle of his baseball career. "Even though it feels like God's not there or he doesn't know what he's doing, he really does," Ishikawa said. "I have to believe that he was just sitting there laughing at me [and thinking:] *If you only knew what's about to come.*"

Needing first-base depth about a month later as Belt struggled with a concussion, the Giants purchased Ishikawa's contract from Fresno after he hit .400 (12-for-30) with three homers, three doubles, and 14 RBIs in his final eight appearances with the Grizzlies. With injuries preventing Morse from doing more than pinch-hitting and serving as a designated hitter, however, Ishikawa found himself in left field, where he started 14 of the Giants' 17 postseason games. It's funny how it works that both Morse and his replacement ended up playing key roles in the postseason.

No Giants player, of course, did more to contribute to ultimate success than Bumgarner. What he accomplished boggles the mind. He pitched a record 52 ⅔ innings in the postseason, finishing 4–1 with a 1.03 ERA in seven games. Two of them were shutouts. In his three World Series appearances, he went 2–0 with a save and an 0.43 ERA. He walked one and struck out 17.

Bumgarner became the third pitcher to earn at least two wins as a starter and work at least three innings of relief in a single World Series. The others were George Mullin of the Detroit Tigers in 1909 and Cy Young of the Red Sox in 1903. Bumgarner tied a record originally set more than a century ago by *Cy Young.* Can you believe that? By the way, in that 1903 season, Young completed 34 of his 35 starts.

Here's another impressive comparison: Bumgarner's ERA was the lowest among pitchers who threw at least 15 innings in a single

Completing a postseason performance for the ages, Madison Bumgarner celebrates after getting the third out of the ninth inning of Game 7 of the 2014 World Series.

World Series since Koufax of the Dodgers registered an 0.38 ERA in 1965. I had the privilege of seeing Koufax pitch many times and can tell you that at least in this World Series Bumgarner was as steady as anyone I've ever seen, including Koufax.

Thus the world discovered Bumgarner's greatness while we around the Giants knew about it for a long time. Half a decade after the 2014 World Series, Bumgarner still commands a certain awe even among his peers. "The grandeur is still there," said Pirates right-hander Trevor Williams after pitching against Bumgarner on September 9, 2019. "I had this game circled [on my calendar] as soon as I found out I was pitching against him because you wake up knowing that you get to face off against one of the greats."

The vanquished Royals maintain extra-special respect for Bumgarner. "If I had to sum him up in one word, I'd say 'bulldog,'" said Jarrod Dyson, a reserve outfielder with the '14 Royals who played for the Arizona Diamondbacks in 2019. "He's somebody who wants the rock, demands the rock, and does what he has to do when he gets the rock. Playing against him, you always looked at him as an ace. Even if he didn't have the velo, he knew how to pitch. He knew how to take what he's got and use it to the best of his abilities. That's what makes him so good. He fears nobody who gets in the box and he goes right after everybody who gets in the box. He's always been a bulldog in my book. You see a guy like that go to war every day and demand the rock. You always say, 'Damn, what would it be like to play with him?' He's one of those type of guys."

Asked to recall Bumgarner's Game 7 effort, Dyson invoked the name of one of the greatest athletes ever. "That's what an ace does. He demands the ball just like [Michael] Jordan on the court," Dyson said. "He wants the ball for the last shot."

Reliever Wade Davis, another 2014 Royals player, spent 2019 with the Colorado Rockies and recalled Bumgarner as being "pretty much the most calm, collected person I've ever seen out there in those situations. He made it look pretty easy." Davis added, "You have to stay calm, you have to stay relaxed. In that big of a game, to throw as many innings as he did and stay relaxed and composed is not easy."

Though Bumgarner admitted after coaxing Salvador Perez's pop-up to end Game 7 that he finally felt tired, Davis still saw a durable opponent. "The last four or five pitches he threw to Salvador, he didn't look like he was overthrowing," Davis said. "Even though we lost, it was awesome to watch."

Then again, it wouldn't be like Bumgarner to show any weakness. "There's a fierceness to this guy that's self-evident," Colorado manager Bud Black said. "Also I think there's a toughness to this guy that I've witnessed from the other side. No doubt there's an old-school, throwback toughness to this guy that I appreciate."

Black's description of being an "old-school throwback" was so accurate. Bumgarner said in a 2016 interview that he would have savored playing when pitchers finished what they started, the designated hitter didn't exist, and batters accepted brushback pitches as being part of the game. "I would have loved to play in the '60s, '70s, and '80s. That's more my speed," Bumgarner said. "I like the way the game is played now, and the game is definitely progressing with tremendous talent. But I like the mind-set of those guys [from previous eras] a whole lot better."

Posey, who has caught Bumgarner in 228 of his 286 career starts through 2019, understands his batterymate's mystique better than anybody. "You could argue that he's one of the few in history—definitely of this generation—who, if you've got one game to win, he's the guy you want on the mound," Posey said. "Not just because of raw stuff, but you know he's going to will himself to win the game. He's proven that over the last 10 years. That's one of those intangible assets that I think people are drawn to. It's really hard to throw numbers on that to be able to value exactly what it's worth."

Bumgarner, who left the Giants for the Arizona Diamondbacks via free agency after the 2019 Season, is such a competitive guy, but as complimentary as it sounds, that might be inadequate. "I would put him in the category of dominator. Simply competing isn't in his repertoire," said Chris Stewart, who frequently caught Bumgarner during 2011, the left-hander's first full major league season. "He wants to go out and dominate every single pitch of the game. He expects to pitch nine innings every single outing without walking or giving up a hit to anybody. That attitude propels him to go out and give the best effort possible, often ending in a positive result for the team."

10

The Dynasty's Top Players, Games, and Homers

I'VE NEVER RELIED much on statistics to judge a ballplayer's value. I want to see how hard he works on and off the field. I want to see how he fits in with his teammates. Of course, I want to see what he does to help the team win. I'm lucky. Throughout all those years that I was clubhouse manager or assisting Mr. Logan, I got to see up close what made a ballplayer tick and also hear what his teammates thought of him behind the scenes. Usually, it was positive but not all the time.

Having a front-row seat, so to speak, for the Giants' three World Series titles gave me a great vantage point from where I could judge how a player was really doing. Listening to manager Bruce Bochy, whose office was across from mine, also taught me a lot. Obviously, I can't repeat most of those conversations, but I think a little bit of Boch comes through in these rankings. And I'm a big fan of intangibles like Hunter Pence giving that big speech to his teammates in Cincinnati before playing the Reds in the playoffs.

So here's how I'd rate the Giants on the World Series championship teams of the 21st century. Just being there is an important quality to me, as you'll see. As the saying goes, the most important ability is availability.

1) Buster Posey
   Seasons: 2009–present

Until recently Posey's career path appeared destined to lead him to the Hall of Fame. He followed up his National League Rookie of the Year award in 2010 with the NL's 2012 Most Valuable Player award, six All-Star team selections, four Silver Slugger awards, and a Gold Glove, among other honors. Even if he retired today, he'd be remembered as the best catcher in franchise history. Guys like Tom Haller, Dick Dietz, and Bob Brenly deserve some consideration. But none of them can match Posey's all-around skills.

2) Madison Bumgarner
   Seasons: 2009–2019

Bumgarner has been so remarkable that other big leaguers regard him with sheer awe. Everybody climbed aboard his bandwagon during and after the 2014 World Series, when he capped a postseason-record 52 ⅔ innings with five shutout innings of relief in San Francisco's Game 7 win at the Kansas City Royals. Unlike other pitchers, I never see him doing crossword puzzles or playing Sudoku or whatever that is. Once he enters the clubhouse, he's all business.

3) Matt Cain
   Seasons: 2005–2017

Cain gets the nod over Tim Lincecum here, though it wasn't an obvious choice. From 2010 to the end of their careers, Cain (41–27, 2.94 ERA, 1.069 WHIP) outperformed Lincecum in the regular season. Both excelled in the 2010 and 2012 postseasons. This span included Cain's perfect game on June 13, 2012, against the Houston Astros. Cain has a below .500 career record mainly because he was frequently injured from 2013 to the end of his career. For those five seasons, he compiled a 19–40 record with a 4.82 ERA and a 1.381 WHIP. Don't let that fool you. He did his job far more often than not.

4) Tim Lincecum
Seasons: 2006–2015

Wasn't he fun to watch? When he got two strikes on a hitter, he didn't pussyfoot around, trying to hit a corner or stuff like that. He went after the hitter, trying to get the strikeout. No wonder he led the National League in strikeouts three years in a row (2008–10). Lincecum's ability was so immense that he no-hit the San Diego Padres in 2013 and '14 even after his talent started to slip. He still managed to strike out more than one batter per inning (641 strikeouts in 615 ⅓ innings) during this period.

5) The Core Four
Seasons: 2010–2015

You can't name just one of them. They must be cited as a unit. All four relievers—Jeremy Affeldt, Santiago Casilla, Javier Lopez, and Sergio Romo—could close games if necessary. But Casilla and Romo were the only ones who did so for significant stretches of time. Lopez was used as a lefty specialist much more than Affeldt was. Yet Affeldt could fill that role. Plus, he could work multiple innings with the best of them. Part of the reason our ballclub has struggled lately is that we haven't found any adequate replacements for them.

Don't let his small frame and boyish looks fool you. Tim Lincecum was a terrific pitcher for us.

6) Brandon Crawford
Seasons: 2011–present

For a few years, it seemed as if nothing got by Crawford. His range to either side was that good. From 2015 to 2017, when he won every National League Gold Glove award for defensive excellence, he seemingly made every play. And what a throwing arm! Everybody wanted to see Pablo Sandoval pitch, but I think Crawford would have made those hitters think a little bit, too. Winning the 2015 Silver Slugger award confirmed his versatility.

7) Brandon Belt
Seasons: 2011–present

Belt rarely was spectacular, but he has remained steady. Looking for more consistency from him, Belt's critics have overlooked his defensive prowess or his ability to extend a plate appearance to eight to 10 pitches, helping exhaust an opposing pitcher prematurely. He's definitely underrated with his defense. He has excellent footwork and he's not afraid to make difficult throws.

8) Pablo Sandoval
Seasons: 2008–2014, 2017–2019

Unlike Brandon Belt, Sandoval possessed a flair for the spectacular—never more so than on the night of October 24, 2012, when he matched a record with three home runs in the World Series opener. Throughout his Giants years, his zeal was evident as he flung his big body toward grounders, took a couple of turns on the mound, and never, ever got cheated when he unleashed his ferocious swing.

9) Hunter Pence
   Seasons: 2012–2018
Whatever Pence did, he was rarely boring. Whether he was racing toward the right-field wall to attempt a dangerous catch or hacking at pitches until he lined one into a gap, he was a genuine winner and leader, as he proved with his oratory during the 2012 postseason. When Pence is finished playing, the Giants would be wise to hire him in some capacity. He could coach part-time, perform public-relations duties, or fill multiple roles.

10) Ryan Vogelsong
   Seasons: 2000–2001, 2011–2015
Vogelsong captured imaginations with his unlikely rise from Japan cast-off to Minor League reject to National League All-Star. He won loyalty with his pitching, which was effective more often than not. It's often overlooked that he was the Giants' leading winner in the 2012 postseason. Man, was he a competitor. When he said, "I'll always be a Giant," he meant it, too. Why else would he turn down a contract offer from the Los Angeles Dodgers to sign with the Giants, even though the Dodgers offered more money?

Jeez, you had me worried there for a minute. At first, I thought you were going to ask me to rank the Giants' 10 best games of *all time*. That would have meant choosing from between great individual performances like Willie Mays' four-homer game in Milwaukee in April of 1961 and games that symbolize outstanding team efforts, such as the clinching games from any of the World Series-winning years. You can't really pick one over the other. Both kinds are great for different reasons.

But selecting the top 10 games from the Giants' dynasty era when they won three World Series titles is less arduous. Here's a top 10 list of games during that span.

1) The First Crown Fits Nicely
November 1, 2010

This wasn't the Giants' most thrilling game of the decade, but it certainly was the most meaningful. Edgar Renteria's seventh-inning, three-run homer off Cliff Lee complemented Tim Lincecum's determined effort in Game 5 of the World Series. Lincecum struck out 10 and yielded just three hits in eight innings while recording his second win in as many World Series starts. The triumph brought San Francisco—the city and the franchise—its first World Series winner since the team moved West in 1958.

2) Bumgarner's Legendary Performance
October 29, 2014

Madison Bumgarner elevated his status from staff ace to legend by finishing Game 7 of the World Series with five shutout innings of relief on two days of rest after blanking the Kansas City Royals on four hits in Game 5. He threw 50 strikes in 68 pitches. Jeremy Affeldt maintained his World Series ERA of 0.00 with two-and-one-third innings of relief. Bumgarner, who stranded Alex Gordon on third base to end this clincher, established a record by pitching 52 ⅔ innings in the 2014 postseason.

3) Perfect Cain
June 13, 2012

Realizing every pitcher's dream, Matt Cain pitched the 22nd perfect game in baseball history and the first ever by a Giants pitcher. Cain struck out 14 batters, equaling Sandy Koufax's mark for most strikeouts in a perfect game. Right fielder Gregor Blanco preserved Cain's perfecto with a sliding catch of Jordan Schafer's drive that led off the seventh inning. Cain provided hints of what was to come by pitching one- and two-hit shutouts in April back-to-back against the Pittsburgh Pirates and Philadelphia Phillies, respectively.

4) Zito Steps Up
October 19, 2012

Trailing the St. Louis Cardinals 3–1 in the best-of-seven National League Championship Series, the Giants notched their fourth of six consecutive victories in elimination games during this postseason. Much-maligned and lightly regarded until this season, Barry Zito struck out six in seven-and-two-thirds innings and retired 11 batters in a row at one juncture to wrest momentum from the Cardinals. You can legitimately argue that he earned his seven-year, $126 million contract in this start and in his next, when he beat Justin Verlander in the World Series opener.

5) Trio For Pablo
October 24, 2012

Pablo Sandoval stole the show in the World Series opener by clobbering three home runs, including two off Detroit Tigers ace Justin Verlander to join Babe Ruth, Reggie Jackson, and Albert

Pujols as the only hitters to accomplish that feat in a World Series game. Barry Zito allowed one run in five-and-two-thirds innings before Tim Lincecum struck out five in two-and-one-third innings of hitless relief. Sandoval proceeded to earn World Series MVP honors by batting .500 (8-for-16).

6) Sanchez Sizzles
October 3, 2010

The Giants needed this victory in the regular-season finale to clinch the National League West title and reach the postseason for the first time since 2003. Jonathan Sanchez not only pitched five innings, but also tripled and scored in the third inning. Buster Posey contributed a home run one inning before Brian Wilson sealed the decision with a perfect ninth inning. During the Giants' on-field celebration, manager Bruce Bochy was seen placing his hands on Sanchez's shoulders to deliver a quiet, personal message. "I'm proud of you," Bochy said.

7) Taxing Night In The Capitol
October 4, 2014

The Giants worked overtime to take a 2–0 lead in the National League Division Series against the Washington Nationals. This 18-inning thriller set records for being the longest postseason game ever both in terms of time (six hours, 23 minutes) and innings (matching the Atlanta Braves-Houston Astros standoff in Game 4 of the 2005 NLDS). Yusmeiro Petit earned the decision with six shutout innings thanks to Brandon Belt's tiebreaking homer in the 18th inning. Belt's 37 postseason games are a franchise record for first basemen.

8) Extra-Innings Resilience
October 9, 2012

The Giants were supposed to roll over for the Cincinnati Reds, who won the first two games of this best-of-five National League Division Series. But despite mustering one hit through nine innings, the Giants, who were stirred by Hunter Pence's passionate pregame speech, scratched across an unearned run in the 10th inning to launch their six-game winning streak in elimination games. San Francisco survived into extra innings despite one hit. But in the 10th inning, a passed ball and an error by defenders who are typically more sure-handed (catcher Ryan Hanigan and third baseman Scott Rolen, respectively) helped the Giants score.

9) Scutaro's Sweep
October 28, 2012

San Francisco completed its four-game World Series sweep of the Detroit Tigers by snapping a 3–3 tie in the 10th inning. Marco Scutaro, who drove in 44 runs in 61 games after being acquired from the Colorado Rockies at the trade deadline, singled to score Ryan Theriot with the go-ahead run. Theriot was San Francisco's designated hitter, having lost his job at second base when Scutaro joined the club. Sergio Romo struck out the side in Detroit's half of the 10th to record his third save of the World Series.

10) Fantastic Freak
October 7, 2010

As the National League Division Series opener, this game began the Giants' three-year postseason run. Tim Lincecum guaranteed that the Giants would get off on the right foot by striking out 14 and limiting the Atlanta Braves to two hits in a brilliant complete-game performance. Cody Ross' fourth-inning single delivered Buster Posey with the game's lone run.

If there's anything more difficult than being a San Francisco Giants batter and hitting a home run, it's ranking the importance of the home runs that they *have* hit. Though the Giants have not been known for their power in recent years, their dynasty era, in which they won three World Series, featured its share of memorable dingers.

1) Edgar's Seventh-Inning Tater
November 1, 2010

Edgar Renteria called a hitters' meeting before a September game at Wrigley Field that year and was moved to tears as he beseeched teammates to capitalize on their opportunity to reach the postseason and give him another shot at performing in a World Series. At the conclusion of his second major league season, Renteria won the 1997 World Series for the Florida Marlins by slapping an RBI single off Cleveland Indians pitcher Charles Nagy in the 11th inning of Game 7. Sure enough, the Giants won the National League West and advanced through the postseason. And in the seventh inning of Game 5 of 2010 World Series, Renteria belted a seventh-inning homer to account for the Giants' scoring in their World Series-clinching 3–1 victory at the Texas Rangers. It led to the Giants' first World Series championship since the franchise moved to San Francisco in 1958.

2) Clutch Uribe
October 23, 2010

Locked in a competitive National League Championship Series, the Giants and Philadelphia Phillies were tied 2–2, entering the eighth inning of Game 6 when Juan Uribe, facing Ryan Madson, smacked an opposite-field line drive to right that barely cleared the wall. Most folks forget that Uribe hit a personal-best 24 home runs that season. The Giants held on to claim a 3–2 triumph that ultimately resulted in their first San Francisco-era World Series title. Uribe, a clutch performer, batted only .149 (7-for-47) in the postseason but made the most of his meager contact by driving in nine runs.

3) Ending A Marathon
October 4, 2014

With an 18th-inning home run off Washington Nationals pitcher Tanner Roark, Brandon Belt broke a 1–1 stalemate in one of the longest postseason games ever in terms of time (six hours, 23 minutes). The Giants' 2–1 win at Washington gave them a 2–0 lead in the best-of-five National League Division Series. The homer was a welcome moment for Belt, who endured three trips to the disabled list—once for a broken left thumb and twice for concussions. These interruptions forced Belt to miss 96 games. But the homer affirmed the Giants' belief that Belt was healthy. In fact, he finished the postseason with a .295 (18-for-61) batting average and 11 walks, the Giants' second-highest total in a single postseason. Barry Bonds set the club record in that category with 27 in 2002.

4) Nice Guys Finish First
October 16, 2014

It was the closest thing to a Bobby Thomson moment that contemporary Giants fans could have experienced. With nobody out and the score tied 3–3, Travis Ishikawa drove a Michael Wacha fastball into the right-field seats at AT&T (now Oracle) Park to seal the Giants' 6–3 victory in Game 5 of the National League Championship Series. The win sent the Giants into the World Series against the Kansas City Royals. This was the same Ishikawa who nearly quit baseball just a few months earlier. During a brief lull in the Giants' raucous clubhouse, beat writer Andy Baggarly observed, "You know that saying, 'It couldn't happen to a nicer guy?'" He let that sentence hang, making it obvious that he was referring to Ishikawa.

5) Most Valuable Homer
October 11, 2012

It seems criminal to rank this homer this low since it was one of the signature moments of the 2012 postseason. But there's plenty of competition. The scene was Game 5 of the National League Division Series at Cincinnati. The Giants were trying to secure their third consecutive elimination-game victory at Great American Ball Park, where the Reds hadn't lost three in a row all season. But Buster Posey proved why he was named that year's National League Most Valuable Player that year. Snapping a scoreless tie in the fifth inning, Brandon Crawford tripled home Gregor Blanco and scored on shortstop Zack Cozart's error. After the Giants loaded the bases, Posey clobbered Mat Latos' 2–2 pitch into the left-field upper deck.

Travis Ishikawa hits a walk-off, three-run home run against the St. Louis Cardinals during the ninth inning of Game 5 of the 2014 NLCS to send us back to the World Series.

6) Morse's Muscle
October 14, 2014

Without this home run, Travis Ishikawa's three-run clout might never have occurred. Michael Morse may well have been the club's purest power hitter, but an oblique injury cut deeply into his playing time. Fortunately for the Giants, Morse was whole enough to unleash a good swing or two every so often. He couldn't have picked a better spot for this one. The St. Louis Cardinals led Game 5 of the National League Championship Series 3–2 and appeared bound to bring the series back to St. Louis, where nothing would be guaranteed for the Giants. Morse erased all apprehension when he batted for Madison Bumgarner to lead off the Giants' half of the eighth. He pulled reliever Pat Neshek's third pitch into the left-field seats to forge another tie and set up Ishikawa's pennant-winning homer. Morse practically sprinted around the bases and answered the fans' curtain call almost immediately.

7) Panda Attack
October 24, 2012

Impervious to intimidation, Pablo Sandoval treated Justin Verlander as few others have treated the Detroit Tigers ace. Sandoval homered three times in the same game, which in this case was an 8–3 Giants victory. Stealing the show in this World Series opener, Sandoval commanded attention with his two-out homer in the first inning that looked as if it had been struck with a two-iron instead of a baseball bat because the trajectory was so low. Sandoval also homered in the third inning off Verlander and in the fifth off Al Albuquerque. Sandoval proceeded to win World Series MVP honors by batting .500 (8-for-16).

8) Ross Is Boss
October 16, 2010

Another postseason series brought another multiple-homer spanking of a future Hall of Fame pitcher. This time it was Philadelphia Phillies ace Roy Halladay, who yielded a pair of homers to Cody Ross in Game 1 of the 2010 National League Championship Series. Ross, who homered in the third and fifth innings, helped dissolve the mystique surrounding Halladay, who pitched a two-hit shutout against the Washington Nationals in his final regular-season outing before no-hitting the Cincinnati Reds in his initial postseason performance. Still relatively new to the postseason scene, the Giants needed a superlative effort from somebody like Ross to fuel their confidence for future rounds.

9) Crawford's Grand Performance
October 1, 2014

The Pittsburgh Pirates and their fans appeared to be going full throttle as the wild-card game against the Giants approached. PNC Park was bursting with a noisy sellout crowd. Then Brandon Crawford silenced the audience for the rest of the evening with a fourth-inning grand slam to back Madison Bumgarner's four-hit, complete-game shutout effort. Crawford joined Chuck Hiller (1962 World Series), Will Clark (1989 National League Championship Series), and Buster Posey (2012 National League Division Series) as the only Giants to hit a grand slam in a postseason game.

10) Pat's At-Bat
July 31, 2010

As the late innings approached, the partisan crowd filling AT&T Park was still waiting for some sign of life from the Giants, who trailed 1–0 and had been limited to three hits by Chad Billingsley and Hung-Chih Kuo through seven innings. Kuo hit Buster Posey with a pitch with two outs in the eighth inning, prompting the Los Angeles Dodgers to summon closer Jonathan Broxton with Pat Burrell due up. Burrell had gone 0-for-3 with two strikeouts, but he connected solidly with Broxton's 3–2 pitch and drove it over the left-center field barrier as the fans shrieked with joy.

11

Tributes to Murph

Ed Bressoud, Infielder (1956–61)
"He had a great sense of humor and a really good work ethic. He did whatever needed to be done. He treated everybody with equal respect and attention. It didn't matter if you were Willie Mays or Ed Bressoud."

Bob Bolin, Pitcher (1961–69)
"A neighbor of mine was a huge Will Clark fan. I tried to get Will's autograph for him. I called the front office for Will's phone number to no avail. So I approached Murph. 'Oh, sure, I will; you betcha,' Murph said. And in no time, he sent me a baseball autographed by Will Clark. I gave it to my neighbor. He thinks I'm the greatest neighbor who ever lived. I think everybody in the league—retired or unretired—knows Murph. He's probably the most well-known guy in sports in San Francisco."

John D'Acquisto, Pitcher (1973–76)
"Having been selected in the first round by the San Francisco Giants in the June 1970 draft, I reported to big league camp in

Casa Grande, Arizona, the following February. After parking my car, I meekly entered the facility through the rear doors, going through the training room. I didn't get far before this tall, skinny guy stopped me. 'Oh, are you John?' he asked. 'I'm Mike Murphy. Let me show you where your locker is.'

We went through the training room and approached the far left corner of a dressing room. On the far right was a guy with his shirt off and wearing his uniform pants. *Oh, my God*, I said to myself. *That's Willie Mays.* I started unpacking until I felt a tap on my shoulder. Of course, it was Willie, stopping by to introduce himself. 'It's an honor to meet you, Mr. Mays,' I said.

"'Don't call me Mr. Mays, John,' he said. 'Call me Willie.'

"'Yes, sir,' I replied.

"'I said, just call me Willie,' he repeated. Willie wasn't done with me yet. 'You like golf?' Mays asked.

"'Yes, s…, uh, Willie,' I said.

"'You like Titleists?' He said as he brought over a dozen new golf balls. They were Titleists, each engraved, 'Willie Mays—24.' 'Let me know if you need any more,' he said cheerfully as he returned to his stall to finish changing into his uniform.

"I met former infielders-turned-coaches Joe Amalfitano and Jim Davenport, who sponsored my first glove and shoe contracts with Wilson Sporting Goods. Wilson's representative, by the way, was Lefty Gomez, the Hall of Fame left-hander. Isn't every day like this? Suddenly, Murph materialized in front of me again. 'Can I get you anything? Do you want anything?' He asked me.

"Actually, Murph already had done enough. Though he gave me little tips here and there about what to do and what not to do, placing me next to Mays was the greatest thing Murph did for me that spring. He put me there to experience sitting next to a star. In essence Murph was saying, 'You'll see how he handles himself and you need to learn from him.'

"After a big night out in South San Francisco eating Mexican food, Charlie Williams, Mike Caldwell, a couple of other pitchers, and I decided to drag race down El Camino Real to the Polo Club in San Mateo. My wife and brother were in the car with me. Charlie ran a red light, but I was the one who got pulled over. I let my brother drive through the rest of the night. The next day I was greeted by Murph in the clubhouse. 'I see you got yourself in a little bit of trouble,' said Murph, who observed that I couldn't make my scheduled court date because we'd be on a road trip. 'Listen to me,' Murph said. 'I'm going to represent you. Get me a bottle of Chivas Regal, and I want you to write a note to the judge who's hearing your case, saying that you apologize for your actions, and it'll never happen again.' When we returned from the trip, Murph approached me and said only, 'Problem solved; problem taken care of.'"

Darrell Evans, Third Baseman (1976–83)
"When he asked me to be best man at his wedding, I was surprised, mainly because he was always a bachelor-type of guy, and we never discussed social things or anything like that. But he had met Carole, and he told me, 'I'm going to get married.'

"I asked him, 'Are you serious?'

"He said, 'Yes, I am, and I want you to be my best man.' It was a big honor and something that came out of the blue. But it's something that makes you proud. It was one of the biggest honors in my life. It was as if the president asked me. I don't think marriage changed Murph, but it sure made him happy and more grounded. It was a small wedding. He didn't make a big deal about it. He doesn't like to make a big deal about anything. During the ceremony I saw a little different side of Murph. I've never seen him as nervous as he was. This was one of those times that I could be right there for him. I also saw his caring. Is there anybody we know who has touched more people? He's touched hundreds, maybe thousands."

Duane Kuiper, Infielder (1982–85)
"One of my favorite Murph stories was he tried to bring food into the clubhouse. He got a guy named 'Jimmy the Greek,' some guy he had met growing up or in his neighborhood. Murph, on this particular night, had Jimmy bring in his special lasagna. Everybody had the lasagna. It was great. We chowed down like we were going to the electric chair. On the way home from Candlestick, there's a freeway exit for South San Francisco as you head toward Foster City and San Mateo, where most of the players lived. There was a gas station off of this exit. And I could tell I was going to crap in my pants unless I got to this gas station, and it had everything to do with Jimmy the Greek's lasagna. I hurried to that gas station. These were the people in line: Jack Clark, Gary Lavelle, Greg Minton, Darrell Evans. We could have had a team picture at this gas station crapper because of Murph's Jimmy the Greek. And we never let Murph hear the end of it. I'll walk by him now and I'll go, 'Hey Murph, are we having lasagna today?' And he'd just burst out laughing.

"I think of his commitment to the Giants and his commitment to his job and really his commitment to the players. In Murph's eyes, the players always came first, and that's not always the best way to keep your job. But the players came first to Murph, and he let you know that even if the player was a difficult player, it didn't matter to Murph. That guy was going to be the most important guy on the team. And he was loyal, man. He worked hard. I don't ever remember being at Candlestick without him. In other words, he always got there before everybody else and he always left after everybody else."

Bill Laskey, Pitcher (1982–86)
"Murph would put out these spreads of food that always made you feel like there was something for each for us. Barbecue weekends with burgers and hot dogs. He put pizzas in the sauna to keep them warm! When he sees me leaving the ballpark late, he'll stop me, make me sit down, and ask about my family. When I played, he'd offer to do our laundry himself or take clothes to the dry cleaners. He's always had that extra touch."

Mike Krukow, Pitcher (1983–89)
"When I played for the Cubs, the legendary Yosh Kawano was there. We all loved Yosh, but he was a bit terse and grumpy. They had a two-clubbie system in Philadelphia. Then I got traded to San Francisco and I was absolutely, completely blown away by Mike Murphy. He thought for everybody in that clubhouse, and there were no superstars in that clubhouse. Everybody was treated the same. The way the clubhouse was set up, that's the way it was set up in New York. It goes back to the Polo Grounds. He is not only a unique clubbie, but a unique human being. When I threw, it was my last pitch—we were in Atlanta—I knew it was my last

pitch. Career over. I felt terrible. Then out of nowhere came this big old hand patting me on the shoulder and this voice saying, 'You did good.'

"Murph is such a gentle soul. He looks after these guys. When former players visit, they're no longer part of that team. Murph is the guy who makes sure that player feels he's still part of that team. He loved his job because he loved the tradition, he loved the politics of the clubhouse, he loved the effort of each player, and he did what he could to make that player's time go well in San Francisco. He is truly legendary. Think of the consistency with which he treated everybody like they were Willie Mays. He complemented the room and the history of that franchise. So many instances where you took him for granted because everything flowed.

"Murph has a kind heart. Each one of the springer spaniels he's had are rescued dogs. And then there are the 'ballpark barnacles.' That's the side of Murph nobody ever saw. Without Murph they'd have died on the street. He treated *them* like they were Willie Mays. There was a guy named Charlie. Nobody knew his last name. And Marjorie Wallace, who showed up hours before every game to greet each player. There was Ed Thomas—'Mr. T.'—a large African American man who had one tooth left. Murph got him a jacket and a badge. He also got him off the streets, same with a couple of trainers, Pete Prieto and Harry Jordan. That's right, the same Harry Jordan whose name was on the award given to the top first-year player at spring training."

Bob Melvin, Catcher (1986–88)

"Murph is a significant part of the Giants experience if you're a player. It's like he's part of the logo. He put me between Willie

Mays and Willie McCovey in the clubhouse my first year at Candlestick. I think he knew with my Bay Area upbringing that it would be off-the-charts cool for me. Murph's the man."

Will Clark, First Baseman (1986–93)
"One day when Scott Garrelts was starting, [manager] Roger Craig warned him that the bullpen was worn out, so he'd have to pitch most of the game, if not all of it. As it turned out, Scotty had kind of a rough day, so he had to 'wear it,' as we say. After the game Roger walked by Garrelts. And instead of saying something supportive or encouraging, Roger said, 'You didn't have it today, did you?'

"Scotty absolutely went ballistic. He threw his chair through the drywall covering the clubhouse ceiling, then took one of my bats and beat a concrete pillar. There's cement going everywhere, pieces of my bat going everywhere, and people running for cover. Finally, he walks out. I had been ducking all of the shrapnel that had been heading my way. Not 10 seconds later, here comes Murph on his hands and knees picking up little shards of bat and cement off the floor. I said, 'You look like you could use some help.'

"Murph never, ever, ever worried about money. Some guys, back in the day, not all, might skip a little bit on their clubhouse dues, and because of not only him being my friend, but also how much he cared for the guys and took care of the guys, I made it really rough on people. You skip out on Murph, I'm going to call you out. So Murph always got taken care of while I was there. Now, since I left, he's told me that guys skip out. To this day, if I find that out, I go call the guys out. Because of what he does and as long as he's been in the game and as much as he's meant to the organization, you don't treat that man like that. Every homestand, *every* homestand, I would come in early, and Murph and I would go to lunch, and we still do. Every time I'm in San Francisco, at least once a homestand, we go to lunch. When you get to be friends like that, it's pretty special. He never lets you pay for anything. He'd fight me over the check, and I'd have to call ahead and sneak money to the employees. It became a little game with us.

"One year, we had this gizmo in the showers that looked like an oversized aquarium. It had a treadmill at the bottom for people doing rehab for leg injuries. I came in early to take Murph to lunch, and the clubhouse kids were peeking around one of the pillars. I asked them, 'What the hell are you looking at?' They pointed to the machine and Murph, who was in there doing backstrokes and stuff. Then he started soaping up. He thought it was a big bathtub. I had to tell him, 'Murph, it's not a bathtub.' That was hysterical. He was kind of my dad away from home. And, he being around the game for so long and me being a baseball guy, a guy who really likes the history of the game, he would always tell me about stuff: Eddie Mathews, Gaylord. You would find out about the history of the game through Murph."

Dave Dravecky, Pitcher (1987–89)

"My first memories of Murph were obviously when I got traded here with Craig Lefferts and Kevin Mitchell from San Diego. When I came to the Giants, my goodness gracious, we were greeted with somebody willing to do everything for us. He was grateful to do everything for us to help us transition. Murph becomes a pretty significant person in your life. He did so much for all 25 of us. What happened after I retired was more significant. On

September 30, 1999, the date of the Giants' last game at Candlestick Park, I was accompanied by my son, Jonathan, who was 14 at the time. Murph overheard Jonathan say that he wanted a baseball for autographing. Suddenly, Murph handed Jonathan this bag. Inside it was 18 new National League baseballs. He got so many autographs—Barry Bonds, Bobby Bonds, Willie Mays, Dave Kingman, Juan Marichal. The list was endless. I was like a kid in a candy store, except the candy was Hall of Famers. Murph was so kind to my son. He really made that trip very special.

"When Murph and I see each other, the first thing he does is give me a hug. He's always genuinely concerned about me and my family. He always invites me to the clubhouse, but that's a sacred place for those [active players]. I'm grateful to be able to call him a friend and to be part of an organization that can call him an icon. He goes on and on in perpetuity. Having to deal with 25 different personalities in the clubhouse, the man's a saint. In a lot of respects, he represents who the Giants are. Murph's the unsung hero."

Don Robinson, Pitcher (1987–91)

"He took care of my boys, Brent and Brad, which was great. They'd meet me in Houston or Atlanta, and he'd have them be batboys. He took care of me, too. I was one of the only pitchers with a bat contract. It was with Louisville Slugger. I signed my first bat contract with Pee Wee Reese for a dollar. I used a model K48—36 inch, 34 ounces for the soft-tossing left- and right-handers and 35 inch, 33 ounces for the hard-throwing guys. My older son, Brad, ever since I was with the Giants and he was 12, has been a Giants fan to this day ever since. He's nothing but Giants. He tweets the

Will Clark celebrates after a run scores during the 1989 NLCS. He was terrific during that series, and he and I remain close.

Giants; he's on their [web] pages. When I went out there last year, I needed to get a Giants cap for Brad. 'No problem,' Murph said. 'How many hats do you want?'

"'Well, how many has you got?'

"'Nine, including the ones for special days and holidays.'

"So I brought back nine hats for my son."

Kevin Bass, Outfielder (1990–92)
"The amazing thing about Murph was that I never saw him lose his patience, even though guys would be coming at him for different kinds of stuff, nonstop. Not once did I see him even frown. If you asked him for a pair of socks, he never said, 'You'll have to wait.' He wanted to do things for you."

Rich Aurilia, Infielder (1995–2003, 2007–09)
"You don't last that long in one place unless you're good at what you do and people like you. All we had to do was walk in and say, 'The best,' and everybody knew you were talking about Murph. He was everybody's grandfather, uncle, brother, dad. I don't think I've ever seen Murph ask anybody for anything. He just enjoyed being around them. You'll never see the level of what Murph did ever again."

Shawon Dunston, Infielder/Outfielder (1996, 1998, 2001–02)
"Murph treated us all the same whether we were Willie Mays or Barry Bonds or Tim Lincecum. I think that's why everybody loves him. He doesn't like publicity. He doesn't like the limelight, even though he deserves it. Not everybody sees this, but he likes to joke around. He'll call us coaches 'couches.' He'll say, 'All the couches,

let's go.' And he tells the best stories. He's like an encyclopedia of players who have come through here. He's seen everybody. He always said that Willie Mays was the greatest player ever, but Barry wasn't too far behind, and he really respected the players on the championship teams. We didn't have boring players. We had professional players, and that was important."

Randy Winn, Outfielder (2005–09)
"First and foremost, I think Murph is a wonderful human being. He has this grandfatherly warmth about him. He's humble and nice, and it shows the minute you meet him. I don't think he has a mean bone in his body. Murph would kill me if he knew I was talking about giving him the nickname 'The Best.' Whenever I see him, I say, 'You're the best.' Rich Aurilia, Mark Sweeney, and Dave Roberts do the same thing. That sentiment was always there; we just started saying it aloud."

Mark Sweeney, First Baseman/Outfielder (2006–07)
"He's easily the best clubhouse guy I've ever been around. And why I say that is: he made the 25th guy on the roster—which I was, the 24th, 25th guy—feel like he was just as involved as everybody else. He brought an atmosphere, a closeness, that you can't equal anywhere else, and it was simple. It wasn't anything that was forced for him. It was just the way he was. He's a parent, he's a friend, he's a confidant, he's a guy who has the pulse of the whole locker room. I love him for many reasons. Honestly, I could talk about him all day long. He was a connection to the history. He was a connection to everything that made you feel good about the San Francisco Giants. If you bring up Murph's name to anyone who's

been in a Giants uniform, it puts a smile on their face. If someone says something bad about Murph, something's wrong. And something's wrong with the guy saying that."

Travis Ishikawa, First Baseman/Outfielder (2006, 2008–10, 2014–15)
"I was looking to get some baseballs for the offseason, just batting-cage balls or a box of balls I could buy. I asked Murph if it would be possible to get a couple of balls for the offseason that I could throw. Well, I came in from the game that night, and there are five dozen brand new baseballs sitting at my locker. He would do anything for you. All you had to do was ask."

Buster Posey, Catcher (2009–present)
"The first time I met Murph had to be spring training of 2009. He was like he is now—he was always going, just had that energetic attitude. There's no way you could do a job as long as he has if you don't have that energetic, upbeat attitude. It's pretty amazing. I've lived here in the offseason for the last few years. I'll come in to the ballpark to work out and I'll think that I'll have the whole place to myself. It's December or January or whatever. Sure enough, Murph's in here doing something. That kind of sums him up. It's in his blood. He can't stay away. This is his home."

Cody Ross, Outfielder (2010–11)
"I'll never forget walking into the clubhouse for the first time after the Giants acquired me, and Murph was the first person I ran into. He acted like we'd known each other for a long time. When I walked in, I had a really awesome, amazing feeling, even though

I didn't know if I'd be able to play because there were so many outfielders. And it all started with Murph, I guarantee you. After we won the division, his face was as excited as anyone's I've ever seen. When we won the World Series, I don't know if it was the champagne in his eyes, but he was in tears. He's the absolute best clubhouse guy I've ever been around. Why? He doesn't ever seem like he has a bad day, although everybody has bad days. His just being there with his smile made you feel better about yourself. What a joy it was to be able to see him every single day."

Javier Lopez, Pitcher (2010–16)
"My first game as a Giant was a series finale against the rival Dodgers. It was an ESPN *Sunday Night Baseball* broadcast, so I got to the yard at around noon. I wanted to be there early, set my locker up, and just get my bearings. I remember walking into the Mike Murphy Clubhouse and seeing the man himself. He was dressed in the same outfit you would see him in today at the park. He was dressed in khaki pants and a black SF logo polo. As I said, I was there to arrange my locker, and Mr. Murph had already done the heavy lifting. He had called the Pittsburgh clubhouse and got my jersey size. Shirt, sleeves, shoes, and socks were lined up and ready to go. He gave me No. 49, and I joked that I wanted 48, which I had worn that season and seasons prior. He looked at me not sure how to answer, even though I knew the answer was no way! A certain animal had taken the Bay Area by storm with his rookie campaign. Pablo 'Kung Fu Panda' Sandoval was not just a player but a merchandising dream, and with that No. 48 was taken. We had a good laugh about it. Also, when I looked at my locker, I was in reliever row. I was next to Jeremy

Affeldt, who would be my lockermate for the next six seasons, and Ramon Ramirez, who like me had been traded. Jeremy, Ramon, and I got along really well along with the rest of the bullpen, some of the best guys I've ever been around. Murph had been around the game his whole life and he knew that treating all the players well regardless of experience is a hallmark of a good clubhouse. To keep it a family atmosphere is critical. That takes 25 players plus countless coaches and staff."

George Kontos, Pitcher (2012–17)
"Sinatra Sundays are a Murph thing. I didn't listen to much Sinatra before I came to the Giants, but on Sundays, Murph got to play whatever he wanted on the clubhouse stereo. That was more than fine with us. Whatever you need to have done, he'll always do it with a smile on his face. He was always the last person to leave the clubhouse, and I was a guy who tended to stay in the clubhouse later than most players, so we had so many conversations. I always sat there and let Murph go on telling stories about the people he has met, like Sinatra. Murph has the most stories to tell and commanded the most respect. He's the epitome of what somebody with the Giants should be like.

"Of course, my Willie Mays story involves Murph. First of all, it was so unbelievable to have a guy like Willie around as much as he was. Anyway, one day I was online and I found a game-worn Willie Mays Giants jersey from the early 1970s. 'You need to get that,' Murph said.

"Somehow I managed to buy it. I wanted Willie to autograph it, but I was very hesitant to approach him. Murph literally grabbed me and led me to his office, where Willie was relaxing. Willie looked at the jersey and said, 'Oh, yeah. This one sold at an auction last week for $55,000.'

"Anyway, Willie signed the jersey, which is now framed and hanging on the wall at my apartment. But one detail is missing. I asked Willie to inscribe the jersey 'To George' to make it a little more personal. Willie folded his arms and said, 'No, I'm not going to inscribe it. I'm going to sign it for you, and you're going to keep it for a few years, and then you're going to sell it and put your kids through college.' Willie actually had my best interests in mind, and I owe it all to Murph. He facilitated the whole thing."

Matt Duffy, Third Baseman (2014–16)
"I wanted to try a new bat model. I wanted only two or three bats. Murph said, 'We'll get you a dozen.'

"I asked Murph, 'What if I don't like them?'

"He said, 'Don't worry about it! We'll get you a dozen.'

"When you're coming up through the minor leagues if you want custom bats, you have to pay for them yourself. For Murph to take care of me like that, I could tell he had pull. He'd find something to do with those bats if you don't need them. It was one of the first eye-opening things I experienced in the big leagues. He's a people pleaser, always about service. Anything you need, Murph would handle it for you."

David Flemming, Broadcaster
"When I first showed up here, I had to earn Murph's trust. Murph is a guy who I think bases just about everything he does on trust—whether you're part of the family, whether you're part of the clubhouse—and he doesn't give you that trust easily. I think maybe a

couple of my predecessors misused that trust a little bit, and so it took him maybe half a year to make sure I was on board. And as soon as you're in with Murph, he will treat you like you're a player, a family member, whatever, for the rest of your time with the Giants. It's been that way for me with Murph ever since those first few months. I didn't just show up and drop a bunch of extra bags in his lap and say, 'Thanks.' If I needed to bring something extra on a trip, I would ask first nicely. One thing about his job is people are always just throwing stuff at him. 'You take care of this, you do this, you carry this, you pack this up for me, you get this gift to somebody else.'

"All this stuff that he gets piled on every day. The nature of it is that sometimes maybe people take him for granted a little bit, and I think all he wanted from me was just a little common courtesy and I think it showed him that I wasn't just taking him for granted. All it took for me really, truly, was to ask him how he's doing when I see him, ask nicely if I needed something extra, a favor, say thank you at the end of every road trip. Little stuff like that with him goes a long, long way. I think he was wary of somebody else coming in and trying to take advantage of him. It's one thing to do a job for that long; it's amazing to do *that* job for that long because that job is never-ending. There's always something—even in the offseason—but especially in the seven, eight months of a season, when you throw in spring training. There's never a moment in any day where somebody's not asking you for something. Just the fatigue of having to do a list of things every single day, every day, for all those years, I give him credit for having a smile on his face and a great attitude all these years because it's not just pure longevity. It's doing that job for that long. I don't know how he's done it.

"It's a special kind of person. It's the kind of person who is selfless, who is willing to put others before him, is willing to do whatever is asked of him, and is willing to be a friend to everybody, even those who aren't that friendly to him. There aren't a lot of people who are like that, and Mike Murphy is one of those people. It's funny because a lot of these guys don't have the sunniest of dispositions. You have to be an optimist to be in that job. You have to give people the benefit of the doubt even when they're not always treating you the right way. He's done that for 60 years. He predicted they would win the World Series before the 2010 season began. Did you ask him how many other years when they didn't win that he predicted that? Well, nobody has a better sense of the group than Mike Murphy. Probably the managers didn't. I don't think anybody else over the years would have a better sense of the emotional pulse of those players than him. Including managers and coaches—and probably most of the time including teammates—nobody else checks in with everybody everyday like he does. So I would trust him on stuff like that.

"Oh, he's still beloved. When people come in from out of town who have known him all these years, they make a point of stopping by over there, not just to see Willie Mays and Orlando Cepeda and whoever else is in there, but a lot of it is to see Mike Murphy. There are so many people around the game when we travel, who ask about him, who want to know about him. To Bob Uecker, Mike Murphy is like Ueck's favorite person in the world. Bob Uecker, who knows everybody, has done everything, and who has done more stuff in this game and outside of this game than anybody in history. Mike Murphy's his favorite guy."

Acknowledgments

A SPECIAL THANK YOU TO THE GIANTS, Larry Baer, Bill Neukom, and the ballclub's outstanding staff. I also want to thank Bob Lurie, Horace C. Stoneham, and Leo "Doc" Hughes, who gave me my first job with the Giants. Eddie Logan, thank you for taking good care of me. And a tip of the cap to all the managers and players who I helped get ready to play this great game.

—MM

The first person I must thank is Julie Pilossoph, and only partly because she's my sweetheart. Before I wrote my first word, she reminded me that Murph was the first person to receive his 2010 World Series ring during the public, on-field ceremony the following April. She gave me the confidence I needed as I took the first steps on my narrative journey.

I'm a little less confident as I continue this summary because I know that I'm omitting people I ought to thank. I will say that at least some of the most helpful folks I talked to—besides interview subjects—included Will Clark, Darrell Evans, Brandon Evans, Pat Gallagher, Mike Krukow, Brad Mangin, and John Shea. They helped reaffirm certain perceptions I developed along the way.

The media relations staffs of the Giants and A's were relentlessly helpful whenever I called upon them for assistance. I shouldn't dwell on my mistakes, but I feel compelled to apologize to five people who took the time to chat with me before every trace of these interviews, written as well as taped, mysteriously disappearing. The Phantom Five are Jeff Brantley, Don Carson, Chili Davis, Michael "Rock" Hughes, and Robb Nen. Darned good group of talkers right there. And I just blain whiffed on Jon Miller. Darn!

Mainly, I remain honored and grateful for being asked by Murph to collaborate with him. There are dozens of excellent sportswriters in the San Francisco Bay Area, many of whom possess more impressive credentials than I do. To be asked by Murph to help him tell his baseball life story was flattering; to actually get it done was a privilege and a pleasure.

I must thank every supervisor I've had at MLB.com. They gave me the assignments that helped me build my career background, which facilitated my ability to work with Murph. Many of the quotations, facts, and features—such as the Giants' all-decade lists—were derived or gathered under my byline in stories I did for MLB.com. I'm deeply thankful for the numerous opportunities the company continues to give me.

—CH